The
HIDDEN HISTORY
of
MCMINN
COUNTY

The

HIDDEN HISTORY

of

MCMINN COUNTY

TALES FROM
EASTERN TENNESSEE

JOE GUY

Charleston · London

History
PRESS

Published by The History Press
Charleston, SC 29403
www.historypress.net

Copyright © 2007 by Joe Guy
All rights reserved

Cover design by Marshall Hudson.

First published 2007

Manufactured in the United Kingdom

ISBN 978.1.59629.349.6

Library of Congress Cataloging-in-Publication Data

Guy, Joe D.
The hidden history of McMinn County : tales from eastern Tennessee / Joe Guy.
p. cm.
ISBN-13: 978-1-59629-349-6 (alk. paper)
1. McMinn County (Tenn.)--History--Anecdotes. 2. McMinn County (Tenn.)--Biography--Anecdotes. 3. McMinn County (Tenn.)--History, Local--Anecdotes. I. Title.
F443.M15G89 2007
976.8'865--dc22
                    2007027883

CONTENTS

INTRODUCTION

T he first railroad built in Tennessee. A governor with two graves. Murder conspiracies. A giant hailstone. An American Revolution in 1946.

In these pages are stories from McMinn County, Tennessee, that cannot be found collected in any other book. While it is true that history runs throughout the stories that I have written about, they are primarily stories. I love stories that are rooted in history, and I have done my best to research and relate the truth and the facts as I found them available, but not knowing all the facts has never kept me from writing, so any mistakes were purely unintentional.

This collection of articles was previously published under my column entitled "Hidden History" from 2004 to 2007 in various newspapers in East Tennessee. Due to the interest I have received from readers across the region, I decided to publish these stories, hoping that they will continue to be enjoyed. It has certainly been a joy researching and writing them.

The demands of a full-time job often hinder the writer, so I am indebted to the following people who provided support, time and their own research that they were kind enough to share with me: McMinn County Mayor John Gentry; the McMinn County Historical Society; historians Kenneth Langley, Bill Akins, Patsy Duckworth, Audrey Dennis, Paul Willson, Rick Lay and Bill Seldon, as well as the late Noel Knox and Sam Sims; Linda Caldwell of the Tennessee Overhill Heritage Association; and both Ann Davis and Travis Haun of the McMinn County Living Heritage Museum. I also owe a great deal to the previous works of the late Charlie Keith, J.M. Sharp and Jim Burn.

Many of the historic photographs for this volume were obtained through the generous assistance of the McMinn County Historical Society, Ms. Audie Dennis of the McMinn County Living Heritage Museum and the Englewood Textile Museum.

This book is dedicated to my good friend and my boss, McMinn County Mayor John Gentry, for the great and many opportunities he has provided me.

And to my wife Stephanie, who says my head is full of useless knowledge…

Chapter 1

MCMINN COUNTY, ONE BRICK AT A TIME

McMinn County lies in the heart of southeast Tennessee, halfway between Knoxville and Chattanooga, halfway between Miami, Florida, and New York City. Historically it was founded on Cherokee land, and the north-south paths through it range from the prehistoric Great Warrior's Path, the Old Federal Road, Lee Highway, to Highway 411 and present-day Interstate 75. Its history is shaped by its location, by its mountain, its fertile rolling valleys and five creeks. These are stories that relate to the area and its far-reaching effects on the region and the nation.

THE HIWASSEE PURCHASE

On February 27, 1819, a group of Cherokee met with Secretary of War John C. Calhoun and signed a much-negotiated land cession treaty. It became known as the Calhoun Treaty, and in the agreement the U.S. federal government bought from the Cherokee all the land between Hiwassee, Little Tennessee and Big Tennessee Rivers lying west of Starr Mountain and the foothills of the Smoky Mountains. Quite suddenly, East Tennessee was opened for white settlement in what became known as the "Hiwassee Purchase."

The Cherokee present, mostly a group of affluent mixed bloods, knew that this agreement would not be popular among their people, but these men also knew that such a land cession was both practical and necessary. Already there were whites living in the area in question. One of the Cherokee, Chief John Walker, operated a farm, store and ferry on the Hiwassee River. A small settlement had sprung up around him that was called "Walker's Ferry," and it seemed to Walker and many other Cherokee that whites were in the habit of crossing the river as much as the Indians were. This was true all across the area, for even in a place named Cades Cove in the Smoky Mountains a family known as the Olivers had built a cabin and started a farm. Chief Walker and the other Cherokee marking the treaty papers that February day believed that if there were already whites on the land anyway, the Cherokee might as well sell the property and at least get paid for it.

Walker had known John C. Calhoun for several years, and wholeheartedly admired the feisty statesman. To Walker, Calhoun had a fire in his heart that reminded the chief of the Cherokee warriors he had known in his younger days. Walker's role in negotiating the treaty, along with his admiration for the secretary of war, caused Walker to rename his settlement on the Hiwassee. Once back home, he began calling the place "Calhoun."

By the following summer, more and more whites were staking claims to what had once been Indian hunting ground. Some of the men had been soldiers in the Revolution thirty years earlier, and had seen the rich land already. Each day a new family arrived, seeking either a place they had purchased legally or some hidden valley or cove they could squat on, hoping to acquire deed and title later on. Several Cherokee decided to move west, across the distant Mississippi to lands that they had been given as part of the Calhoun Treaty. But many remained, having adopted white culture. Many farmed or operated businesses like Walker, and lived peacefully with their white neighbors.

It became clear by the end of the summer that new counties would need to be formed out of this new land. Tennessee Governor Joseph McMinn, a man always interested in land himself, began to express his support for the development of new counties and the appointment of county government.

And so the new settlers waited through the summer, talking among themselves about what needed to be done. When the legislature convened in the fall, there would be much business to attend to.

The Tennessee Legislature was still meeting in Murfreesboro that November day in 1819 when several items of interest were brought before the elected officials. For six days in the legislature, discussion of lines and county names ensued. In southeast Tennessee, two counties were decided upon, and lines were drawn out from the existing Roane County. These two new counties would cover the territory of the entire southeast corner of the state, where Tennessee, North Carolina and Georgia came together.

The northeasternmost county was considered for a name, and after some discussion, it was decided to honor past President James Monroe by calling the county Monroe County. This county's line would run from Roane County up the Tennessee River to the mouth of Cowee Creek, then west to North Carolina, then southwest along the Carolina line to Georgia, then north along the line that would be set for the second new county.

Calhoun, McMinn County's first settlement on the Hiwassee River. Cherokees and whites are buried alongside each other in its historic cemeteries. *Photo by Stephanie Guy.*

Discussion then ensued regarding this other county. What would it be called? Already a U.S. president had been honored. What about the present governor of Tennessee, Joseph McMinn? Such a name would indeed honor the man who had supported this land acquisition in the first place, and so it was done.

The new county would be known as McMinn County, and its line would run southwest from Roane County to a point equally distant from the Cherokee town of Tillassee on the Little Tennessee River and the town of Hiwassee on the Hiwassee River, then along Monroe County south to Georgia, then west to the Tennessee River, then north along the river to the Roane County line.

Under the Acts of 1819, Chapter Number 7, this legislation was approved by the Tennessee Legislature on November 18, 1819. That day, McMinn County was born. Places for county government were also designated, which for McMinn County would be the home of Major John Walker in the little hamlet of newly named Calhoun on the Hiwassee, at least until a more suitable seat of county justice could be designated. The sheriffs of the counties were ordered to elect officers from the militia districts, with the

Homesite of Return Jonathan Meigs, agent to the Cherokee, on Main Street in Calhoun. *Photo by Stephanie Guy.*

able-bodied men from McMinn to compose the Sixty-seventh Regiment of the Tennessee State Militia.

Over time, other counties called Polk, Meigs and Bradley were borne of McMinn. From "furs to factories," as the Tennessee Overhill Heritage Association says it, McMinn County has come a long way from its humble beginnings as Cherokee hunting lands. From wilderness cabins and dirt trails to multimillion dollar industries, modern roads and debt-free government that is the envy of many other counties in the state, McMinn is the "little county that could." Like any solid Southern matriarch, she has gotten only more beautiful with age, and her people still gather around to celebrate and honor her.

THE CLEAGES: EAST TENNESSEE'S FRONTIER BUILDERS

I have trouble keeping my Cleages straight. And to make matters worse, I still have trouble pronouncing the name correctly. In case you have the same problem, it's pronounced "Clegg." Some historians say the name was originally spelled this way, up until the family changed it with the addition of an "a" and an "e" around the time of the Civil War. According to an article by Penelope Allen Johnson in the January 21, 1934 edition of the *Chattanooga Times*, the name Clegg comes from the old English word "clough," meaning a break in the hillside.

Keeping your Cleages straight appears to be a common problem with historians in East Tennessee. In almost every generation, there are Thomases, Alexanders and Williams.

Samuel Cleage was the first of the clan to travel into East Tennessee. The youngest child of Revolutionary War Patriot Alexander Cleage, young Samuel showed an inherent talent for business. Becoming a skilled building contractor in Botetourt County, Virginia, Samuel began moving southwest after his father's death in 1822. As he traveled through the valley of Virginia and into the newly opened lands of East Tennessee, Samuel would stop by large farms and sell the owner, or better yet the owner's wife, on the idea of moving from the standard log cabin into a spacious brick home, which Samuel would build with his highly skilled Angolan slaves. After being paid in additional slaves or livestock, he and his family would move on. By the time he arrived in the Sweetwater Valley of McMinn County, Samuel Cleage was a wealthy man.

And it was here, just below the settlement of Mouse Creek (later Niota), that Samuel put down roots and built his home in 1825. This formidable structure still stands on Highway 11; it has survived 180 years as a testament to the Cleage brick-making methods. Samuel took his son-in-law Thomas Crutchfield as a business partner, and the firm Cleage and Crutchfield built numerous buildings in East Tennessee, many of which still stand. At one time, the firm had contracts to build nine courthouses in East Tennessee, and until the Civil War it was the leading contracting business in the region. Samuel's son Alexander was also active in local affairs as a builder and banker, and some historians claim he was the one who eventually changed the spelling of the name from Clegg to Cleage.

Truly the first "developers" in East Tennessee, the imprint of Clegg/Cleage and Crutchfield is still visible, especially in Athens. Of the buildings constructed by the firm still standing in McMinn County are the Clegg house, the Boggess house, Mars Hill Church, the historic Van Dyke house, the Crutchfield house, the old Rice house, the Keith house, the Harris-Turner house, the old Hiwassee Railroad office building (the first railroad in Tennessee) and the old Planters Bank–Thomas Crutchfield–Alexander Cleage house. Other buildings that were built but no longer stand are Cleage Hall, the Athens Hotel, the Bank of Tennessee/Saliba Sanatorium and the first McMinn County Courthouse. The structures that still remain all have a similar type of brick that is characteristic of the Cleage-Crutchfield method of construction.

Mars Hill Church, built by Alexander Cleage in 1836. Its bricks were made by slave labor, and some still bear the marks of the slaves' hands. Cleage bricks were of high quality, as the slaves themselves were master craftsmen. *Courtesy of the McMinn County Historical Society.*

The building business would continue with Samuel Cleage's grandsons, William and Thomas Crutchfield Jr. According to Goodspeed's *History of East Tennessee*, these men would later move to Chattanooga, where they would build the Crutchfield House Hotel in 1847 on the site of the present Read house. This was the premier hotel in Chattanooga, and it operated through the Civil War as a hotel, General Grant's headquarters and as a hospital. On January 22, 1861, William, a staunch Unionist, had a heated exchange with future Confederate President Jefferson Davis in the hotel lobby. It was only by the intervention of his Confederate-minded brother Thomas that a physical altercation did not break out. William worked very closely with the occupying Union forces, often at the outrage of his own family.

William would serve as a congressman after the Civil War, and Thomas was twice the mayor of Chattanooga. Thomas lived at his spacious farm above Chattanooga, called Amnicola, from which the present Amnicola Highway takes its name.

Old Samuel Cleage died in McMinn County on July 20, 1850, and is buried in the family cemetery at the intersection of Highway 11 and Highway 305 (this plot is surrounded by private property). While only Cleage descendants remain in McMinn County today, the family was one of the most prominent in East Tennessee and McMinn County for most of the nineteenth century.

THE CLEAGE SLAVES

Samuel Cleage, the itinerant contractor who traveled into the Tennessee valley from Virginia in the 1820s, is generally credited with the construction of several historic homes and buildings in East Tennessee, especially in McMinn County. While it is true that Cleage was the driving force behind his construction business, it is important to remember who, in fact, was actually performing the labor.

Besides livestock and gold, Cleage was often contracted to be paid in slaves after having completed a house or building. Many of Samuel Cleage's Angolan slaves later adopted the Cleage name when they obtained their freedom, and several black families in East Tennessee still trace their lineage to these Cleage slaves. Cleage was a wealthy landowner besides being a builder, so he used his slaves almost exclusively as bound workers in his construction business. One of the duties often exclusively regulated to the slaves was brick making.

By the time Samuel Cleage was involved in building, the art of making brick had been around since 3500 BC. Essentially, nineteenth-century brick making involved five steps: winning or digging the clay, preparation, molding, drying and firing.

East Tennessee is well known for having the natural clay useful for brick production. Once dug by the slaves (normally in the fall), the clay was exposed to the weather so that the winter freezes could break the clay down, remove unwanted impurities and allow it to be worked by hand. In the spring and summer, water was added and the clay was worked by the slaves' hands and feet in large open pits until it obtained a smooth consistency and most of the rocks and sticks were removed.

The clay was then taken to the molding table, where the slave designated as brick molder directed several assistants in the process. A skilled brick molder would work at the molding table for twelve to fourteen hours a day, producing 3,500 to 5,000 bricks in a day. A clot of clay was rolled in sand and "dashed" into a sanded mold, which prevented the clay from sticking. Once the clay was pressed into the mold, the excess clay was removed from the top of the mold with a flat stick. Molds ranged from single to six bricks at a time, but single brick molds were often desired because even the slave women and children could be employed in carrying the "green" bricks from the table to the drying area. The "green" bricks were then stacked and dried for about two weeks.

Once most of the moisture had dried out, Cleage's slaves stacked the bricks in a kiln, or clamp. Rows of bricks were built up to construct tunnels, which were filled with wood and set on fire. For two to five days the bricks were cooked, with the slaves feeding the fires and getting very little sleep. After the bricks cooled, the slaves removed them from the clamp and sorted them by their degree of quality, the best being chosen for the building's outside walls. Bricks that were closest to the fire sometimes received a natural glaze from the sand that fell into the flames, and were used in the interior courses of the walls. Some bricks that would be left with a salmon color were only slightly underfired, and made for good insulation in the inner parts of the walls. Bricks that were over burned, cracked or warped were called clinkers and were saved to be used in garden walls or paths.

Several structures that Cleage's slaves built still stand in McMinn County: the Samuel Cleage house, Keith mansion, the Van Dyke house, the Rice building, the Cate house, the Hiwassee Railroad office and Mars Hill Presbyterian Church. The fact that these buildings remain after over 150 years is a testament not only to the Cleages, but also to the Cleage slaves who performed the hot, backbreaking labor of brick making and masonry. I recently inspected the Hiwassee Railroad office and Mars Hill Church with

Hiwassee Railroad Building, built by Cleage slaves in 1836, pictured in 1936. *Courtesy of the McMinn County Historical Society.*

Travis Haun, curator at the McMinn County Living Heritage Museum. Travis believes the bricks in these two structures, which are near downtown Athens, were indeed locally made by hand, with a fairly high degree of skill.

All across East Tennessee today are families who can trace their roots to the Cleage slaves through names such as Cate, Ferguson, Witt, Johnson and others. These people can take pride in the fact that their ancestors, though enslaved, were the skilled builders of some of East Tennessee's most enduring homes and buildings. These historic structures, lasting through the rages of time and use, are a testimony to the unnamed hands that labored in their construction.

Finding the County Seat of Justice

Sitting at his house in December 1819, Sheriff Spence Beavers must have wondered why he had accepted the post in the newly formed county named McMinn. He was the first sheriff, and if his job as a law officer wasn't enough, he had just received word that his duties were about to become even more difficult.

The previous month, in November, the Tennessee Legislature had passed a private act creating McMinn County, and Beavers's office was one of the first to be filled, per the Tennessee Constitution. He had now learned that other offices had to be filled, as well as a decision made on the location for a county seat of justice. Beavers read over Chapter Number 7 of the Acts of 1819, and saw that he was instructed to "hold an election at the places appointed for holding courts…on the first Friday and Saturday in May next, for the purpose of electing filed officers for the militia…and the militia of McMinn County shall compose the sixty-seventh regiment, and be attached to the seventh brigade."

The legislative act went on to say how the regiments were to be divided into companies, and that the companies would elect their own officers. These companies would be created according to the different militia districts in the new county, which at that time composed what are now McMinn, Polk and Bradley Counties.

History tells us the militia companies were later organized for each militia district. These militia districts, which would in 1834 become civil districts, were also the source for other governmental and judicial offices. In each militia district was a justice of the peace. Four times each year, the justices from the militia districts would meet and hold McMinn County Quarterly Court. Two years later, the state legislature instructed the justice of the peaces of the militia companies to hold an election "for the purpose of electing a fit and proper person from each of said captains companies as a commissioner to fix upon a suitable site for said seat of justice in said county of McMinn."

At the time only two sites were being considered: the small river settlements of Calhoun and Columbus. Both settlements were relatively old or were near an old Cherokee town, and both had access to the Hiwassee River at Calhoun to the west and at Columbus farther upriver to the east near Starr Mountain. Each location must have been duly considered, for the legislature gave specific instructions on how to acquire the properties and lay off the streets of whichever site was selected. The commissioners were also charged with the construction of the very first public buildings in the county, those deemed most important by the legislature for the operation of county government: a courthouse, a prison and stocks on the public square. Until such buildings were completed, the temporary seat of justice would stay at Calhoun. Columbus was eventually taken in as part of Polk County in the 1850s, and later disappeared altogether. Only a historical marker on Highway 411 just north of the Hiwassee River Bridge makes note of the one-time contender for McMinn County's seat of justice.

As time went on, there arose an issue of accessibility for the citizens of McMinn County regarding their county seat of justice. Calhoun was a long wagon ride from the northern parts of McMinn, and an even longer

In this early photograph of McMinn County's seat of government, Athens is pictured with dirt streets surrounding the courthouse and businesses on the downtown square. *Courtesy of the McMinn County Living Heritage Museum.*

walk. Rumors also persisted that the surrounding country would be further divided up into new counties with the purchase of more Indian lands. The idea of the seat of justice being on the county's southern boundary didn't make much sense.

So the commissioners set out looking for another location, a place that was more central and easily accessible from all areas of McMinn. Today, it might seem clear why the "friendly city" of Athens was eventually chosen. It is quite an attractive and cozy place, almost a picture-perfect location for the county seat. But this is romanticizing things a bit. To the commissioners who chose the site, the characteristic of beauty was far down the list. In a largely agrarian economy, the use of land was viewed from a more practical standpoint. According to the Tennessee Private Acts of 1822, Chapter Number 194, passed on August 23, 1822,

> *Whereas the commissioners appointed in pursuance of an act of the General Assembly of this State, passed at the last session, have agreed and pitched upon a site for a seat of Justice in McMinn County, as near the center thereof as an eligible site can be procured, and where as the land upon which said seat of justice is placed is vacant and unappropriated, and quite poor and barren, being valuable only for the waters and timber; therefore...*

That the register of East Tennessee shall issue a grant for the one half of the following tract of land…for the establishment of a seat of justice in said county…that the said land is very poor, and valuable only for water and timber upon the same…and that the said town shall be called and known as Athens; which said site is hereby established and made permanent seat of justice for said county forever.

Chapter 2

THE CIVIL WAR IN MCMINN COUNTY

N o other location in the South was as equally and openly divided by the difficult years of the Civil War as East Tennessee, and this was especially true in McMinn County. The majority of McMinn Countians voted to stay with the Union, although McMinn County had the second highest slave population in East Tennessee. These are a few tales of the experiences of war, most of which relate to the stories of common people whose lives the war touched, and sometimes ended.

When the Calhoun Confederate Became a Lincoln Lover

It is said that she was quite the storyteller in her old age. Her name was Ms. Elizabeth McElreath (later Elizabeth Elbin), and she lived much of her life in Calhoun in McMinn County. Her home was near the old Saulpaugh Mill, where Oostanaula Creek empties into the Hiwassee River. During the Civil War, she was a staunch Confederate, a descendant of John Sevier, a cousin of the "Raider" General John Hunt Morgan and the wife of a Confederate major.

When Union troops occupied the area around her home, Ms. McElreath took every opportunity to harass the "Yankee" soldiers. Her sharp tongue and loud voice made her disdain of the Federals very clear, and she began to earn quite a reputation.

After some time, the Union soldiers had enough of Ms. McElreath's abuse, so they paid her a visit. But after the soldiers burned some buildings and destroyed some property, the outspoken lady was not to be silenced. In her anger, she poured barrels of syrup out in her yard and broke jars of fruit against the trees while taunting the Union soldiers to "lick it up." When her tirades grew worse, the local Union commander had Ms. McElreath arrested and sent to Nashville to be tried.

The judge in Nashville heard Ms. McElreath's case, and questioned her about her Confederate sympathies and animosity toward the Union troops. He also asked where she was staying while in town. Ms. McElreath replied that she was "staying at the best hotel in town at the expense of the Federal Government." Her niece, trying to keep the peace in front of the judge, offered to pay the bill, but Ms. McElreath vehemently refused to do so because "we are guests of the US Government and it will have to pay the bill. We were brought here and it will have to pay the hotel bill." Luckily for Ms. McElreath, the judge was quite amused at her tenacity and sharp tongue. He only admonished her to go back home to McMinn County, to try to get along with the occupying soldiers and to stop being so bitter.

Not to be deterred, Ms. McElreath decided to appeal to none other than President Lincoln for compensation of her loss of property during the Union raids. She traveled to Washington and made her way to the White House.

Of course, the presidential office was full of people waiting to see the president. Not to be outdone, Ms. McElreath waited three days for an appointment. When her time finally came, she approached Mr. Lincoln in his office. For once in her life, she paid the president enough respect to allow him to speak first. Lincoln walked over to her, patted her head and said, "My child, what brings you here?"

Ms. Elizabeth McElreath told the president of her losses and frustration with the Union forces. He listened carefully, and then said, "You must remember that this is war, and everything is out of balance and abnormal, but so far as it is in my power everyone who has suffered unjustly will be paid."

Afterward, Ms. McElreath spoke of how sad the president seemed, and how she felt that, had he lived, she no doubt "would have been paid for all the devilment those Yankees did me."

Meeting Lincoln must have had quite an effect on this die-hard Confederate lady from Calhoun. Years later, she spoke fondly of meeting her inveterate enemy, saying, "I went there hating him but came away loving him."

A Dead Soldier on Courthouse Square

Few, if any, photographs remain of the original McMinn County Courthouse, or at least the first courthouse that occupied the present square in downtown Athens. A log structure that was located on the north side of the square was

Photo of Athens taken around 1890, from the "fort" on Depot Hill where both Union and Confederate troops maintained an artillery emplacement during the Civil War. *Courtesy of the McMinn County Living Heritage Museum.*

initially used as a courthouse in the early days of Athens, but it is certain that a brick courthouse building stood on the square during the Civil War.

This building was the scene of at least one minor skirmish during the years of the War Between the States. Another occurred when the opposing blue and gray sides were holed up in the courthouse area and the old depot, exchanging fire along White Street. There were no major engagements in McMinn County, and so we lay claim to these smaller skirmishes when we talk about the Civil War in our area.

The firefight around the courthouse that I had previously read about was given more light in a presentation I recently heard by Bill Akins, former McMinn County historian. Mr. Akins related an entry from the memoirs of Joshua William Caldwell, who was a witness to the courthouse skirmish. These memoirs are on file at McMinn County's E.G. Fisher Library.

As Mr. Caldwell relates, McMinn County was like much of East Tennessee in that it exchanged hands numerous times during the Civil War. It must have been common for the citizens to take a good look around when stepping out of doors each day, because their fortunes could change in a heartbeat, depending upon what color coats were worn by the army patrol that was in town that day.

Mr. Caldwell, in his memoirs, tells of such a day during the war when a detachment of Confederates rode into Athens to assault some Federal soldiers who were using the courthouse as their headquarters. He writes,

"At one time there was a garrison of Federals in the courthouse, and one day while we were at dinner, a company of ragged Confederate cavalrymen charged into the square surrounding the temple of justice." Musket fire rang out, and at some point the action grew serious enough that several townspeople took refuge from the gunfire. The gunfight continued, and the "big zip, zip of the big musket balls continued until the Confederates were repulsed."

Afterward, the obviously young Mr. Caldwell, along with some other curious onlookers, investigated the scene of the small battle. He wrote, "Then I went down with some of our friends and had an attack of the shivers. The first thing we saw in the square was a huddle of old rags and an old slouch hat. When we went to this we found it was a dead Confederate soldier." The poor condition of the soldier made quite an impression on Mr. Caldwell: "I have in these later years seen many tramps and beggars; duty has now called me to the abode of the most abject and squalid poverty; but never have I seen so ill clad, so utterly unwashed in person and in dress as this dead soldier."

Athens and McMinn County are proud of its downtown area, especially the area of the courthouse. It is still a picturesque location, even with the urban sprawl that is drawn westward by Interstate 75. And while the courthouse beside which the Confederate soldier died is gone, as is the building that followed it, our present courthouse is still the center of our county, both as a seat of government as well as the center of most of our legal affairs. It is regarded with envy among the citizens of neighboring counties, and it is in many ways a symbol of our county.

And so, while we come and go through the Athens downtown, transacting our business in and around the courthouse today, it is difficult to imagine horses tied up in front of downtown businesses and hotels, livestock roaming through the streets and bluecoats and rebels fighting to the death in the hot, dusty lanes and alleyways. And it takes a bit of imagination to look through the eyes of Joshua Caldwell to see the dirty young soldier, unknown and ragged, lying curled up in death on the street beside the courthouse.

THE VAN DYKE LEGACY

One of McMinn County's most historic homes was recently damaged by fire; it is a large brick structure right under the public's nose but largely hidden from view. On the hill behind Eastside Shopping Center and the American Cinemas, surrounded by overgrowth and kudzu, is the dark, imposing home built in the 1830s that is known as Prospect Hill. It was the home of one of East Tennessee's most notable citizens, Thomas Nixon Van Dyke.

T.N. Vandyke was immersed in history as soon as he was born in 1803, at Fort Southwest Point in what is now Kingston in Roane County, where his father, Thomas, was an army doctor. His grandfather was Judge David Campbell, a close companion of John Sevier who was involved in much of early East Tennessee history, including the short-lived state of Franklin.

After receiving an education in Pennsylvania, T.N. Van Dyke went to Alabama, where he practiced law and was soon appointed to be the clerk of the state legislature. Van Dyke was known as an efficient clerk and attorney, and he found himself practicing law in Athens in 1833.

It was around that time that Van Dyke acquired the sizeable tract of land on the town's southern outskirts and constructed the large brick structure on the hill overlooking Oostanaula Creek. The home was remarkable for the time; it was one of the largest in the area, with terraced gardens and large oaks and sycamores encircling it. Its walls were of solid brick, some eighteen inches thick, baked on site from hand-dug clay acquired by slaves from the nearby hillside. After a few years in Athens, Van Dyke was appointed as director of the Branch Bank of Tennessee. He was a principal figure in bringing the railroad to Athens, and in 1854 he was elected chancellor of the bank.

As the Civil War broke out and McMinn Countians faced almost constant dangers from both armies, Mrs. T.N. Van Dyke saw a campfire burning on the hill near the Van Dyke Cemetery. She approached and asked which army the soldiers were with. From the darkness came the reply, "Colonel Nathan Bedford Forrest, ma'am, at your service."

Van Dyke was a staunch Secessionist, and suffered much as a result. He swore not to shave until the Confederacy won the war, and at the end of the conflict had a long, white beard that had to be thrown back over his shoulders. Four of his sons (William, Richard, John and Thomas Jr.) volunteered for service in the Confederate army. Only William survived the war, as both Richard and John were killed in the area of Darksville, Virginia, and Thomas became ill at Cumberland Gap and died in Athens. T.N. was arrested by Union authorities as a Confederate supporter in 1864, and was sent to prison in Ohio, where for a time it was rumored that he had died. While Van Dyke was away, a red-haired Union general passed through Athens, and finding the women at Prospect Hill in a deplorable situation, provided them with passes to stay with kinfolk in Illinois. The general then took up residence for a time at the house, which must have infuriated Van Dyke, as the general was William T. Sherman. Van Dyke was eventually released, and returned to Athens in 1866.

After the war, Van Dyke maintained his plantation and was involved in numerous civic affairs, including serving in various appointments by the state legislature. He was a trustee for the Tennessee Hospital for the Insane, tried cases before the Tennessee Supreme Court and was commissioned chancellor four times between 1878 and 1880. In 1873, Van Dyke sold the land surrounding his family's cemetery to the Town of Athens; this land later became Cedar Grove Cemetery.

T.N. Van Dyke died in March of 1891, at the age of eighty-eight, in Rome, Georgia. He was brought home and buried in the family lot, within sight of the home he had built on the hill in Athens. And that home still remains, surviving the years of war and neglect, and even a late fire, to remain a symbol of one of Tennessee's most prominent citizens.

FORREST, SHERMAN AND A "LITTLE STRANGER" AT ATHENS'S PROSPECT HILL

A recent article about the old Van Dyke home, known as Prospect Hill, behind the present American Cinemas in Athens has produced a great amount of attention. Local historian and author Bill Akins presented me with even more interesting information on the Van Dyke family.

Published several years ago by the East Tennessee Historical Society (journal number 28) is a copy of a memoir by Mrs. Anna Marie Deaderick Van Dyke, wife of William Van Dyke, the only son of T. Nixon Van Dyke to survive the Civil War. Mrs. Van Dyke was twenty-five years old when the war began, and in her memoir she records much of her experience while a resident of McMinn County.

Well do I remember the first time I ever saw the Yankees. True they were Tennesseans—but they wore "the Blue." 'Twas on a September afternoon of '62, that the alarm was given—that the Yankees had driven their wagons into the corn field & were sweeping everything—That corn meant food for man and beast—& although there were only females about the house—We determined to have a small share of that corn…We succeeded in saving several loads of corn—and being very weary from the new experience—I had seated myself on the front porch steps—and had scarcely gotten a good breath when two most inoffensive looking "blue coats" walked up and asked for something to eat. I tried to rise, but sank back—seeing my agitation, one sneeringly remarked, "Madam, we are not horned animals!" hastily and almost unconsciously I replied Sir, to me you

Prospect Hill, the home of McMinn County's notorious Confederate supporter, T. Nixon Van Dyke. *Courtesy of Jimmy White.*

are more horrible than any horned animal. In after days I got over this terror. But, "they hungered, and I gave them meat."

Athens was often raiding ground—today the Confederates, tomorrow the Yankees—One afternoon my husband (a Confederate officer) dashed in to spend a short time with his family—these homecomings were always attended with so much danger…After an almost sleepless night, I looked out early the next morning, to see everything ablaze with campfires…I aroused Mr. Van Dyke—explained the situation—told him to dress and prepare for a flight while I reconnoitered. Taking with me a sister-in-law we ran about a quarter of a mile…until we reached the encampment. In the gray dawn of the early morning—we could scarcely discern the color of the uniforms—and hesitantly I inquired "Whose command is this, gentleman?" Not receiving a satisfactory answer I approached a commanding figure who seemed to be marshalling his forces—"Won't you tell me whose command this is?" The answer came…"Madam, it is mine, Nathan Bedford Forrest's Brigade."

With almost fleetness of the wind we returned to Prospect Hill—my husband was standing beside his horse, ready to leap into the saddle… Suffice it to say he retired "decently and in order with General Forrest."

Soon after this, General Sherman pressed his way into our little village—I have not time nor disposition to enumerate all the inconveniences, annoyances and outrages, that this acquaintanceship of six weeks with Sherman's army brought us. Will only say the house was ordered burned—the order revoked—and it was taken for headquarters for the officers.

After her father-in-law's arrest by Federal forces, Ms. Van Dyke and her two children were sent out of Athens under a flag of truce to the Confederate lines, and she headed for her father's home in Jonesboro. But this trip would have its own reward in store for the Southern lady as she passed through Strawberry Plains: "On the second day of our journey—we met a flag of truce going to Knoxville, on official business, commanded by my husband—For nine months I had not seen him nor hear one word from him. Perhaps you can imagine the meeting—after a Happy half hour the flags were ordered to move on—for war is a tyrant."

Mrs. Van Dyke also records the many hardships that were facing the citizens of McMinn County:

I have lived on little, and then on less—have lived three months solely on Irish potatoes and corn bread—have been nauseated on the fancy coffee of dried apples—sweet potatoes, and rye…have seen my children sicken with the angel of death over them, and no resources at hand…Have knit socks by the dozens—have sent to the front boxes of bandages and lint…Have spent all night in cooking for retreating soldiers.

Mrs. Van Dyke's memoir is a window into our history during the Civil War, and her experiences tell us much about day-to-day life, especially as she relates her own experience as an expecting mother during the war years: "During the siege of Vicksburg—with mind torn and distracted, for my precious ones were there, a little stranger came to my home unattended by nurse or physician."

THE BABE OF THE CONFEDERACY

John Robert Jackson Morris was eighty-eight years old when he died April 8, 1942, at his home along the Athens-Englewood Road. Evans Funeral Home performed the funeral arrangements at the Morris home, as was still the custom, followed by the burial at Cedar Grove Cemetery in Athens. That year, World War II raged in Europe and the Pacific, and one wonders what Robert Morris thought of the conflict that enveloped the world, for

Robert Morris was an old soldier himself. A Civil War veteran, one of the last to take his leave of his earthly duties, Robert Morris had a noteworthy military career. Noteworthy, it seems, due less to his service than to his age.

Born May 7, 1853, Robert had barely turned ten when the Confederacy's Fifty-ninth Tennessee Mounted Infantry was organized, made up mostly of southeast Tennessee Confederates seeking to avoid the coming Federal occupation. Robert's father, Isaac Morris, along with his grandfather Jesse K. and brothers Jesse and John, had already left their farm in the Goodsprings community and enlisted in General Cook's detachment in the Fifty-ninth and "shouldered their guns and marched away." Robert would later say that the lure of adventure was too great for him to remain at home, and that he "was lonesome and wanted something to do." So the boy stole away and followed the troops to their rendezvous in Morristown. His father was not pleased, and administered a "sound whipping" to his son with the orders to go back home immediately.

But young Robert was not so easily deterred. He spent two whole weeks hiding from his father by posing as a helper on the baggage wagons, until he mustered enough courage to face his father again. He said later that this encounter was also in the presence of General Cook. The general was so impressed with the boy's valor that "he put his arm around me and said 'You are a soldier, but a very young soldier.' He gave me a gun and 100 rounds of ammunition." As Robert was only a boy, a uniform was out of the question, forcing him to wear a homespun jacket and jeans.

Mr. Morris was known in his later years as "Uncle Bob," and was considered by many as the "baby of the Confederacy" because he was believed to be the youngest soldier in the War Between the States. Uncle Bob was recalled as enjoying any opportunity to relate his experiences in stories and tales that listeners found entertaining. Much of what he claimed was related in his obituary in the *Daily Post Athenian* in April 1942:

> *"Uncle Bob" told of a skirmish that soon followed and was separated from his company and was pursued by 100 Yankees. He crawled through a cane break, and by swimming the French Broad river he escaped the Yanks. After this trying experience he decided to go home but he was no sooner there until he changed his mind. So he set out on foot for the front, traveling mostly at night and rejoining his father's regiment near the Tennessee-Georgia line. General Cook put him at once on picket duty.*

His adventure, it seems, was not quite over, as Robert had found his company about to enter the Battle of Chickamauga:

In the capacity of picket duty, guarding the line, according to "Uncle Bob," he fired the first shot that opened the memorable battle of Chickamauga. As an incident of the famous and very red engagement of the war, "Uncle Bob" said his father was the gunner of the cannon called "Whistling Dick," and that this piece of death cut down hundreds of men and horses in the battle. According to "Uncle Bob" he also participated in the Battle of Vicksburg.

According to local Civil War historian Kenneth Langley, much of Morris's claims are valid. In the book *Tennesseans in the Civil War*, the following men are mentioned: Private Robert Morris in Company H, Private Isaac Morris in Company A and Jesse K. Morris in Company H. The Fifty-ninth, also called (Eakins) Tennessee Battalion, included Captain James B. Cook's regiment under the command of Colonel John M. Van Dyke of Athens. In the Morris family file in the McMinn County Historical Society there is a letter written to historian Reba Boyer dated June 18, 1879, that says Isaac Morris was not in the 1860 census and that he joined the Confederate army at Firestone (in the area of Mecca Pike) in McMinn County, and that James C. Morris also joined from Firestone. Jesse K. Morris joined in Athens, and Robert Morris was in the same regiment.

There was no doubt of "Uncle Bob" Morris's stories in April of 1942. His obituary was listed under the following notice: "FUNERAL SET FOR ROBERT MORRIS, BELIEVED TO BE THE YOUNGEST SOLDIER IN THE WAR BETWEEN THE STATES."

Chapter 3

STARR MOUNTAIN

Rising to some two thousand feet through Polk, McMinn and Monroe Counties, Starr Mountain's history is as rugged as its hollows and peaks. These are some stories about the mountain's places and its people.

Caleb Starr's Tennessee Mountain

I attended a cemetery dedication recently, that of the old Cooper Cemetery east of Etowah, in the Conasauga Valley alongside Starr Mountain. And as I listened to the dedication remarks spoken so eloquently by preservationist Marvin Templin, I looked to the mountain where the fog hung heavy and low. As cattle called in the distant field, I thought of the man for whom the mountain was named, and of his home that once stood on a nearby rise only a few hundred yards away.

Caleb Starr was born in 1758 in Chester County, Pennsylvania, of Quaker ancestry. At some point in adulthood, Caleb migrated to North Carolina, and about 1775 he came into the Tennessee country, along with future Governor Joseph McMinn. Some sources say the two knew each other well.

In 1797, Caleb is listed as a hireling to Ellis Harlan, a fellow Quaker and a well-known trader to the Cherokee. Both are listed as whites living in the Cherokee lands in "Persons Residing in the Cherokee Country, Not Natives of the Land in 1797" in a letter by Agent Silas Dinsmore to Governor Sevier. It is probable that Starr had worked for Harlan for quite some time, as Harlan had been a trader, and at times a spy, for many years. Harlan had married the daughter of Nancy Ward, Katherine Kingfisher, and fathered a half-breed girl named Nannie about 1777.

Although he was a bit older than she, Caleb Starr must have taken notice of Nannie while working in her father's trading business. Caleb would have

It was here, in the Conasauga Valley, that Caleb Starr established his huge farm on the lands allotted to his Cherokee wife. The mountain was named after him. *Photo by Stephanie Guy.*

seen her often, and he also would have seen much of the Cherokee lands in his travels and visits with the Indians. It is likely that he first saw the rich lands in the Conasauga Valley while he was employed with Harlan. When Nannie Harlan was seventeen years old, Caleb took her as his wife in about 1794.

Around 1800, the year her father died, Caleb and Nannie moved into the Conasauga Valley underneath the shadow of the Unicoi Mountains and built a two-story frame house on a small rise at the foot of the ridge. Starr continued to work with and for the Cherokee, while at the same time building up a rather large farm. On July 11–12, 1810, Caleb is listed on the records of Indian agent Return J. Meigs as having been compensated for blacksmith work ($10.75) and for building two looms ($16.00) for the Cherokee. On a receipt dated November 1, 1815, of the United States government's Cherokee annuity payment for the years 1813 to 1816, $36,000 was paid to Return J. Meigs, United States agent to the Cherokee nation, which was to be dispersed among the Indians. The receipt was signed by Caleb Starr, among other leaders, indicating his position of importance as a member of the nation. Not long after, Caleb would be involved with both the Treaty of 1816 and the Treaty of 1819. But it was the Treaty of 1817 that secured Caleb Starr in the ownership of his ever-growing plantation.

By the eighth article of the Treaty of 1817, the United States agreed to give a reservation of 640 acres of land to each and every head of an Indian family residing on the east side of the Mississippi River. Each reservee was to have a life estate for himself, but the treaty provided that should the owner remove voluntarily from the land reservation, the right of ownership was to revert back to the United States. When the Hiwassee Purchase was made in 1819, the Indians' reservations had precedence over the subsequent land sales. Caleb Starr's reservation alongside the mountain was recorded as section nine of the fractional township Range 1 East on the Conasauga Creek, in newly formed McMinn County, Tennessee. By that time, the Starrs held the 640 acres and worked the farm with around one hundred slaves.

Caleb Starr had by that time already established himself and was raising a large family on his beautiful valley farm. He was so recognized that those who settled nearby began to refer to the towering mountain not as Chilhowee, but as Starr's Mountain.

For about thirty years, the Starrs lived on their farm. Fourteen children were born there: Mary Jane, James, Thomas, Ruth, Ezekiel, Sarah, George, Joseph McMinn, Rachael, Nancy, John, Alexander, Deborah and Ellis. Only John and Alexander did not live to adulthood. Of all the children, James seems to have been the most flamboyant and controversial. It was he

Caleb Starr's two-story house stood here, on the slight rise behind the trees. He remained here until his voluntary removal to the Cherokee reservation in Oklahoma with his wife and extended family. *Photo by Stephanie Guy.*

who convinced President Andrew Jackson to give 640 acres to certain white settlers moving into the area. James became a member of the Treaty Party, which advocated total tribal removal, and with other members he signed the controversial Treaty of 1835, which would result in the total removal of the Cherokee in 1838.

Like his sons, Caleb Starr seems to have supported emigration, as did many of the mixed bloods. The Anti-Removal Party, led by John Ross, was supported mostly by full bloods. Several years before the Trail of Tears, some of Caleb's sons, including Ezekiel and James, had already relocated to the lands west of the Mississippi. After the removal was complete, members of the Removal Party were hunted down and killed. James escaped the first round of bloodshed, only to be killed later in 1845.

By the time he sold his Conasauga Valley farm and traveled the long trail to the West, Caleb was almost eighty years old. Like others who supported removal, Caleb may have seen the futility of fighting with the determined policies of Andrew Jackson, or he may have simply believed there was a better life awaiting the Cherokee out West. He and Nannie died in 1841 and 1843, respectively, and both were laid to rest in the Going Snake District, Cherokee Nation, Indian Territory (now Adair County, Oklahoma).

Some sources say that Caleb Starr's grave lay unmarked, and I am unsure if it remains so today. His original home is also gone; having fallen into disrepair, it was torn down in the mid-twentieth century. But I do know that rising almost two thousand feet, and following a twenty-mile course over Monroe County, the eastern edge of McMinn County and into northern Polk County, is an everlasting monument to Caleb Starr, a mountain forever named for the man and the life he made in the Conasauga Valley.

THE LEGEND OF BUSTER DUGGAN

On April 2, 1914, a passerby made a disturbing discovery in Conasauga Cemetery east of Etowah near Starr Mountain. A new grave had been disturbed; a hole was dug down to the coffin, and a fire had been built in the hole. The man put out the fire and repaired the grave, and told his story to his neighbors.

Few were surprised at the incident, for the grave that had been violated was that of William W. "Buster" Duggan, who had been buried only the day before. It was one last insult to a man who was known as both a devoted friend and husband and a coldblooded murderer by people from McMinn, Monroe and Polk Counties.

Buster was born in 1879 on Mecca Road in the Conasauga Valley beside Starr Mountain. His family later moved to Alabama, where he grew up. Buster was a typical young rebel rouser, a slim and handsome man with a passion for hunting, shooting, fighting and drinking. A faithful friend, he was cruelly violent when crossed. One of the first men he killed was his own father-in-law, who had tried to have Buster arrested at his own wedding. Buster served a little time for the murder before breaking out of the Gadsden, Alabama jail in 1897. He then decided to return to his family homeplace in Tennessee.

But trouble was always a part of Buster's life, almost as if he were addicted to it. In 1906, he was involved in a dispute where he killed two men, one of whom was a former friend, in Monroe County near Mount Vernon. For eleven months, Buster eluded attempts to arrest him, traveling back and forth along the secluded trails between McMinn and Monroe Counties, and living with his cousin Sam Duggan when he broke his leg in a fall from his horse. Buster even dug up a recently buried body from the Eleazer Cemetery and burned the dead body with his own coat in an attempt to fake his own death, but the ruse failed. At times, he would visit prospective witnesses in the dead of night, attempting to intimidate their

This grave was found disturbed on a cold morning in 1914. Someone had dug into the fresh grave of Buster Duggan and built a fire inside it to show their fear and hatred of the outlaw. *Photo by Stephanie Guy.*

testimony. Finally, Buster was apprehended by the Monroe County sheriff on the Mount Vernon Road after almost shooting a deputy.

His trial was held in January 1908. Although a large amount of evidence was presented against Buster, his accomplished lawyer, Nobe Peace, was able to gain a mistrial. The rural people along Mecca Road on the McMinn-Monroe County lines became even more fearful. And events continued to support their fears.

Later in the same year, Buster's cousin Sam was killed by a police officer in Englewood who was trying to arrest him for disturbing the peace. A few months later, Buster's brother, Hugh, was shot down in Englewood after an argument. Buster, his heart full of vengeance, hunted the two men who had killed his brother and cousin. He often entered the men's homes when they were away, forcing the wives to cook him food and sometimes even lying in the men's beds to ensure that his intentions were clear.

Buster was retried in September of 1908 on the murder of the two men in Mount Vernon, but was again represented by the able Nobe Peace. This time, there would be no doubt: the jury found Buster not guilty. Rumors spread about Buster Duggan, who was seemingly able to murder men without having to answer for it. Even Buster's kinfolk spoke of him in nervous tones. Law officers refused to approach him outside of a public street. No one knew what he might do next.

Five years passed, and again Buster took a man's life during a card game one day on the roadside on Mecca Pike. Again, he fled to the hidden caves and coves of Starr Mountain to evade any attempt to arrest him. He would occasionally visit some family, who although terrified would give him food and clothing in order to allow him to move on. Emboldened by liquor, he sometimes amused himself by shooting at people walking to church at Stephensville. And no one seemed to have the courage to confront him.

Feeling indestructible, Buster established a moonshine still on the southern end of Starr Mountain, in the territory of another "tough" named Bart Boring. When Buster believed Boring's son had told some deputies about the still, Buster ambushed him and killed him. He even went so far as to ransack young Boring's house and threaten his wife, intending on making himself the "king of the mountain." But Buster had seriously misjudged the Boring clan.

Before long, Starr Mountain was covered with men every bit as reckless as Buster Duggan. He received a message that said, "If you stay on this earth, I'll kill you." With the tables turned, Buster had few places to hide, and he never traveled the mountain trails without several loaded guns. He made a rare visit to his house on March 2, 1914, and while he was on his porch washing his face for dinner, he was shot and killed by an unknown assailant hidden in his barn. McMinn County Sheriff T.B. Ivins followed the killer's trail to the top of Starr Mountain, but it was there he called off the search. The men who were able to kill Duggan were men to be reckoned with, and Ivins was no fool.

No one was ever indicted in the murder of Buster Duggan, or in the burning of his grave. But his legend is still whispered about along Mecca Pike, and by the mysterious smoke that occasionally drifts over Conasauga Cemetery.

THE HOTEL ON "BALCONIES OF STONE"

Its advertisements were in newspapers all over the Eastern United States— an open invitation to its "medicinal waters, magnificent scenery" and "dry, invigorating atmosphere." At two thousand feet above sea level on the side of Starr Mountain near the McMinn-Monroe County line, White Cliff Springs Hotel was heralded as the Saratoga of the South.

As mineral springs were once considered a naturally occurring medicinal resource, a small hotel and cabins were built alongside such springs on Starr Mountain by Major Joseph Peck around 1850, overlooking the Conasauga Valley area of Monroe County. An advertisement in the *Athens Post* said the hotel's springs were "Tonic, Diuretic, and Alternative, and have proved very effacious in relieving diseases of the Liver, Kidneys, and Stomach, and have acted as a sovereign remedy in Chlorosis and Dysmenorrhea." J. Harvey Magill of Mouse Creek (later Niota) purchased the hotel in 1860 and expanded it. It survived the Civil War intact, although the remote site attracted many of the "outliers" and bushwhackers that prowled the region. By 1869, the hotel's business was booming.

But a fire destroyed the structure in 1869, only to be rebuilt by Magill to an even grander scale in 1871. Photographs exist of a three-story hotel with verandas enclosing all sides that gave visitors a spectacular view of the mountain and valley below. The new hotel had over one hundred rooms, with a large ballroom on the bottom floor, along with a barbershop and a spacious lobby complete with a piano and organ. A poem penned by A.M. Tuttle spoke of White Cliff with a "view kaleidoscopic" and sitting on "balconies of stone."

Tuberculosis and yellow fever were common illnesses during those times, and it was believed that the dry, thin mountain air at resorts like White Cliff provided relief, as well as a location far removed from the heat of the Deep South. Of course, the springs were believed to be medicinal as well, and patrons routinely dipped in the covered pools that held the fresh mountain waters. These springs were said to be rich in "chalybeate, alum, sulphur, freestone, iron, and magnesia."

From all over the South, Northeast and Midwest, visitors left their trains at Athens and Mouse Creek, riding in wagons and carriages the twenty miles to "hack stations" at the foot of Starr Mountain. "Hacks" were small carriages suited for the steep mountain roads and driven by experienced local men who knew the dangers of the ascent. Remnants of the old hack roads still exist, as does at least one hack station at the intersection of Highway 39E and Highway 310. After the harrowing ride up the side of Starr Mountain, the visitors could finally relax after their daylong journey. In 1895, the trip was made considerably shorter when the rail line was extended from Athens to Tellico Plains, and patrons could debark at White Cliff Station at the base of the mountain.

It must have truly been a vacation for the times. The cool mountain air would drift over the mountain, and the quiet forest was relaxing for visitors to the area. Patrons took hikes over both Starr and Black Mountains, stopping off at the Bowers home, Bullet Creek Falls and the nearby cliffs of

Providing 115 rooms at the top of Starr Mountain, White Cliff Springs Hotel earned the nickname the "Saratoga of the South." *Courtesy of the Englewood Textile Museum.*

The springhouse at White Cliff Springs Hotel. The spring waters were believed to cure numerous diseases in the mid- to late 1800s. The springhouse was also a place for sweethearts to "court" each other, sometimes even carving each other's initials in the springhouse posts. *Courtesy of the Englewood Textile Museum.*

white granite, from which the springs took their name. Another source of amusement to the patrons was the rare appearance of the haggard hermit Mason Evans, who resided in a cave on the other side of the mountain and would creep around the hotel looking for food. An indication of the importance of the hotel was the fact that a Bell telephone line was run up the mountain by 1893 to provide communications back to Athens. At times, up to four hundred guests enjoyed White Cliff's amenities.

Business continued for the prosperous Magill, until his death from injuries sustained in a fall down a flight of stairs at the hotel in 1897. The building and springs were then purchased by R.L. Everhart, who ran it as a boardinghouse. In the early twentieth century the property was owned by Jack and Harry T. Burn of Niota, and was used for a time as a hunting club. But the old building finally fell into disrepair, and was torn down around 1937. The property remains in the possession of the Burn heirs.

Today the forest has covered up the hotel site on Starr Mountain road. Only a few bricks remain, as do the stones that surround the springs of what was once one of the most heralded vacation sites in America.

WILDMAN OF CHILHOWEE

Being confined in a jail cell must have been a nightmare to Mason Evans. The deputies who brought the ragged man into Athens that day in 1890 had been forced to bind him securely to keep him from escaping. Word quickly spread around town that Mason was in the county jail, so a line of curious people filed through the crude building, anxious to look upon this man-thing they had heard so much about. The Wildman, they called him.

Mason cowered in the far corner of the jail cell, drawing his knees up to his chest. His eyes were wide and fearful as the steady stream of strange people murmured and pointed at him. The cold walls of his prison were something Mason was not accustomed to. He was used to the free air and open range of Starr Mountain. It had been his home for many years, and he did not remember ever living anywhere else but in the cave on the mountain. In Mason's dim mind, he only felt fear at being in a strange place that he did not understand.

In fact, it had been some forty years since Mason Evans threw off the confines of ordinary life. Tales abounded regarding the old hermit, most of which revolved around him once having been a handsome local schoolteacher, well known and liked in the communities around the McMinn-Monroe County lines. But a scorned love affair had caused him to lose his mind, people said, and Mason had gone off to Starr Mountain, turning into a ragged shell of a man. He'd taken refuge in a small rock shelter that was known locally as Panther Cave, just below the top of the mountain, overlooking the Conasauga Valley. He lived off what food he could steal from the local residents, who often took pity on him and left food out for him near their barns and corncribs. Still, some residents feared the ragged man who made strange sounds and wore only rags and an old dirty hat. Sometimes the fearful and angry citizens aroused the authorities to Mason's thievery, and so it was that deputies had found the old man, bound him and brought him to jail.

It wasn't the first time he'd had trouble with the law. On the other side of Starr Mountain from Panther Cave stood White Cliff Springs Hotel. The large resort and its mineral springs were known all over the Southeast. It was said that the springs had medicinal powers, and people traveled from far and wide to visit the imposing frame structure that stood out from the top of the mountain.

But a fire destroyed the hotel one night only a few years after the War Between the States ended. Mason had often lingered around the hotel, often because he was allowed to eat the leftover food from the guests' meals. With the cause of the fire so mysterious, many assumed it was the Wildman who had burned the hotel to the ground. Mason had been captured, but in his deranged state could offer no clues as to whether he was guilty. He'd managed to escape back to the mountain, and since the owner of the hotel pitied him, no formal charges were ever filed. White Cliff Springs was eventually rebuilt to an even grander scale than before.

Although he was a perpetual loner, Mason had an occasional pet that he kept with him. An old, featherless, bony rooster was his companion for several years, but when he was seen without it, people assumed Mason had eaten the bird when he was unable to find food during a sparse winter.

On that day in 1890, as the crowd of people passed through the old jail, Mason simply huddled in the corner. Men and young boys pointed and whispered, and ladies covered their faces at the stench of the derelict. A photographer came and took a picture of Mason. A newspaperman was also there, writing down a sensational story about the capture of the noted hermit and thief. But Mason took little notice. In his childlike mind he was terrified and lost. Finally, evening came and the crowd fell away from the curious and destitute old man. A deputy came and set a bag of food down on the straw floor. Mason ate ravenously in the darkness, glad to be alone again.

Sometime during the night, Mason escaped. He roamed the mountains for a few more years, but old age and his haggard life took their toll. Some say he froze to death on the mountain, or in a shack he sometimes slept in

Mason Evans, the hermit of Starr Mountain. His tragic story remains a distinct part of eastern McMinn County lore. One of his haunts, Panther Cave, is still visited by hiking and historical enthusiasts. *Courtesy of the Englewood Textile Museum.*

on his brother-in-law's farm. Still others say he died after being arrested, cold and alone in a jail cell. He was buried at Hickory Grove Church near the Mount Vernon community in nearby Monroe County.

For years afterward, people still spoke of him. Tales were told and retold of a parent or grandparent who had left food out for the strange old hermit. Long after his wanderings, his encounters with the law and his nights spent on Starr Mountain, only Panther Cave remains to tell the tale of Mason Evans, the rejected lover, the ragged lonesome man, the Wildman of Chilhowee.

Chapter 4

THE STRANGE AND THE SPOOKY

No collection of stories would be complete without the ghosts, spirits, tales and otherwise strange places, people and things that make up a community. These are all rooted in fact, some more than others, and relate a different, and sometimes a darker side, to the McMinn County area.

GOVERNOR JOSEPH McMINN'S OTHER GRAVE

Joseph McMinn, former governor, Indian agent and McMinn County's namesake, rests in a quiet grave in Calhoun, Tennessee. McMinn was sixty-five years old when he fell ill and died quite suddenly at his desk on November 17, 1824. A Presbyterian, McMinn had requested to be buried in the church graveyard, which was done according to his wishes.

As was often the case, Joseph McMinn's grave was not marked, and it remained unmarked for years. After so long, there were fewer and fewer people in Calhoun who could remember where the former governor had been laid to rest. With Athens becoming the largest town in the county, less and less business was done in Calhoun, and less attention was paid to Joseph McMinn.

After a while, Athens had established itself as the county seat, and would even grow to rival Knoxville in both population and industry in the years before the Civil War. And as time would have it, the people of Athens began to take an interest in local history, and they began to take an interest in Joseph McMinn.

In the 1870s, as McMinn County approached its fiftieth birthday, someone had an idea: Why should poor old Joseph be forced to lie in an unmarked grave in lowly Calhoun? If Athens was the center of McMinn County in all things, then Joseph McMinn should be afforded a better gravesite. Soon it was decided: they were going to move Joseph McMinn's body to Athens.

The gravesite intended for Governor Joseph McMinn at Cedar Grove Cemetery in Athens. Calhoun residents, however, did not agree with parting with the deceased governor's remains. *Photo by Stephanie Guy.*

Cedar Grove Cemetery was chosen, as it was the resting place of many prominent McMinn Countians. Joseph would be among good company there. Even today, the site that was chosen can still be seen, an enclosure made of marble on the cemetery's west side. The name "McMinn" was even carved into the marble. Steps were constructed, as well as a podium in order to make a big to-do once Joseph's remains were relocated there. Athens had many jewels in her crown, and to have McMinn County's namesake interred in her soil would certainly add one more jewel.

The day came to remove Joseph, but those who went to Calhoun with such lofty intents ran into a problem. No one could say for sure where the venerable governor rested. The Athenian group heard many a "I think its right here" and "I heard he was right over there," but no one could agree. Without a headstone, the Athenians were, as you might guess, between a rock and a hard place.

Finally, someone remembered an elderly gentleman who they thought was alive when Joseph McMinn was buried. He was sent for and asked the question.

"Yes," he said, "I was about twelve years old and recall it well. Why do you want to know?" Excited at finding their solution, the Athenian men told

Governor Joseph McMinn's grave in Calhoun, Tennessee. The obelisk marks the location of the governor's remains. This cemetery is the oldest in McMinn County. *Photo by Stephanie Guy.*

him of their great plan to relocate Joseph to a better neighborhood. The old man turned sour.

"Then I shall not tell you," he said. "The good book says not to disturb a grave, and I shall not allow it to be done."

No amount of encouragement would sway the old man's decision, and after some time, the Athenian men went back to Athens, and Joseph stayed in Calhoun. The McMinn plot in Cedar Grove would remain McMinnless.

Several more years passed before Governor Joseph McMinn received the obelisk that now covers his grave. He was more fortunate than another historic figure, Daniel Boone, who died and was buried in Missouri. The state of Kentucky decided it deserved the Boone remains, and sent a party of men to disinter the remains of Daniel and Rebecca Boone and bring them to Lexington, where they remain today.

Unless you speak to the people in Missouri, who say the Kentuckians robbed the wrong graves, and that old Daniel still rests in his original place.

But not Joseph McMinn. Thanks to an old man's scriptural beliefs, Joseph McMinn was never disturbed, and eventually got his tombstone placed on his grave. And for Joseph's sake, we hope it's in the right place.

A Grave Mystery at Cedar Grove Cemetery

For years, the story has been told by older residents of Athens, Tennessee. Pointing their finger toward the lonely old grave in the city's Cedar Grove Cemetery, the tale was always much the same: "Here," they would say, "is where an unknown Indian chief is buried."

The grave, lying in the oldest part of the cemetery, is covered with broken stones that were once part of a solid concrete covering. A blank headstone still rises over the head of the grave, and old newspapers tell of the grave being robbed in 1925. For years, rumors have floated around about the grave, and much speculation has occurred about its unknown inhabitant. With the Cherokee removal having taken place in the late 1830s, the grave would have to be at least 170 years old.

But hidden history is a funny thing. It can lie sleeping, much like a grave, for decades before it is called forth. Recently, this was the case involving the mysterious chief buried in Cedar Grove.

Local historians Bill Akins and Kenneth Langley have completed a project to write a comprehensive book about McMinn County during the Civil War. As part of their work, Mr. Akins and Mr. Langley have read numerous personal memoirs and interviews of Civil War veterans, some written several years after the war.

One such interview found in a local family scrapbook by Mr. Langley was that of Alford M. Hacker, who was possibly the last Union veteran to pass away in McMinn County. In the newspaper article from the *Chattanooga Times* on July 28, 1935, the ninety-five-year-old Mr. Hacker makes reference to his father, Alford M. Hacker Sr., who was a stagecoach driver in and out of McMinn County during the years of the Cherokee removal. Mr. Hacker recalled that his father was driving the coaches in 1836–37, when General Winfield Scott was directing the "rounding up" of Cherokee who had refused to migrate westward. One of the Cherokee, an old "chief" named Deerhorn, escaped the roundup near Cleveland and climbed aboard Mr. Hacker's stagecoach. As the old Cherokee was ill, Mr. Hacker drove him to the post house in Athens where the Living Heritage Museum now stands. That Mr. Hacker would take pity on the old Indian is understandable, as his Grandfather Julius Hacker had been involved in working with the Cherokee to construct the Old Federal Road through eastern McMinn County in 1806. Deerhorn's illness must have been quite severe, as he died at the post house and was buried in Cedar Grove Cemetery.

Upon discovering the old newspaper clipping, the connection of the Deerhorn story to the grave in Cedar Grove was the first thing on Kenneth Langley's mind. "I believe it's Deerhorn," said Mr. Langley. "It's just about got to be."

And so it appears a longstanding legend and mystery has been solved. The resident of a lonely, unknown grave in Cedar Grove is now known, along with its connection to the terrible removal of a native people from their home, and a small cup of mercy given a sickly, old Indian so many years ago.

WHAT'S OUT IN BROCK HOLLOW?

Many a Halloween has passed with a spooky tale told to frighten children and adults alike. It's simply part of the "holiday," and it shows our strange desire to be voluntarily scared out of our wits. While I've always enjoyed the standard yarns involving vampires, werewolves, witches and ghosts, the local stories were always just a little spookier to me. I guess it was the fact that even though I really didn't believe the stories, it was always a little unnerving to think that they might have happened, and that they might have taken place somewhere close by.

Such is the story of Brock Hollow (properly pronounced "holler"). This narrow stretch of road just south of Englewood has long been a source of fright, and a tale has been woven over the years that may or may not be true. I'll let you decide.

The mysterious grave of an Indian chief in Athens's Cedar Grove Cemetery. It is believed to be that of an elderly Cherokee who died in Athens during the Trail of Tears in 1836. *Photo by Stephanie Guy.*

What is now the west end of County Road 480 was once the original site of "Old Englewood." The small mill town of Eureka was located about two hundred yards from the intersection of Old Etowah Road (County Road 500) along Chestuee Creek, and as early as the Civil War was printing its own "script" or currency for use by the mill employees in the company store. As was the nature of a mill town, the people worked long, hard hours and often applied their leisure hours to hard living. Drinking, gambling and fighting were some of their favorite sports.

It was supposedly just such activity that led to this story. One night, several of the men were involved in a poker game. A stranger who was new to the settlement was winning over big, which caused the others to suspect him of cheating. They plied him with homemade liquor, hoping to get him too drunk to play, but he only got luckier. Well after midnight he had completely won out, and with a sneer on his face he took his winnings, a pocketful of gold and silver pieces, and left. He headed out into the darkness to the east on Brock Hollow Road, where there was a well-known brothel at the next intersection at Old Federal Road.

But the stranger never made it. The next morning, he was found robbed and murdered, hanged from a tree along the roadside. With no known identity, he was laid to rest in an unmarked grave, the location of which was lost to time. The murderer or murderers were never identified, although a large amount of suspicion was placed on the men who had lost the poker game.

Time went on, and saw Englewood moved to its present site on the railroad. The brothel on Old Federal Road was closed down and disappeared. The little mill town faded away, leaving only the owner's home and part of the old mill still standing. Years passed, but the tale was not forgotten. And how could it be? For more than one local citizen told of strange nighttime occurrences along Brock Hollow Road.

Some told of seeing something hanging from the huge oak that still stands by the road today. Others saw lights moving through the lonely woods, and still others reported seeing someone walking through the quiet hayfields. Even a sheriff's deputy claims to have passed a strange man walking along the roadside, apparently searching for something. When the officer turned around to investigate, the man was not to be found.

Is it only a tale? Or is it the stranger, searching for his stolen poker winnings, or maybe for his lost grave? Of course, the rational explanation is to blame it all on the fog that often settles in the narrow valley, or perhaps on someone's idea of a practical joke. But there's only one way to know for sure.

If you're driving along Brock Hollow Road on a dark and foggy October night, you might come upon someone walking. They say he'll be a bit pale, with a forlorn look on his face. If you want to know what he's doing, just stop and ask. But if you're like most people in the area, the hair will stand up on the back of your neck and you'll just keep on driving, hoping you'll make it to the end of Brock Hollow Road.

INSIDE THE McCULLEY MAUSOLEUM

I met recently with a group of historians and took a tour of Cedar Grove Cemetery in Athens, where many of the movers and shakers of early McMinn County are buried. I, along with Paul Willson, Rick Lay, Mr. and Mrs. Jerry Smith, Kenneth Langley, Patsy Duckworth and Bill Seldon, walked among the stones that held such names as Magill, Fisher, Willson, Ivins, Horton and Cooke, discussing the relevance of each, who was related to whom and other interesting tidbits of history. But the most out of the ordinary story was told by Rick Lay as he unlocked the doors of the only mausoleum in Cedar Grove and allowed me to venture inside.

Sometimes a thirst for a good historical story makes you do strange things.

The mausoleum is small, only about nine feet wide and twelve feet long, made of split-faced granite blocks. It is, we think, one of only two privately owned mausoleums in the county, the other being at Green Hill in Etowah. It was constructed in the 1890s for the two souls whom rest inside: Joseph and Miriam McCulley. I ducked into the cool, dark interior and peered through the cobwebs at the names and dates on the two marble-enclosed crypts that lie silent against the back wall, one on top of the other. I must admit, it was a bit unnerving to be inside with Rick outside holding the keys. But I was learning to trust Rick, and hoped he wouldn't decide to lock me in as a joke. I tried to ignore the sound of those keys jingling in Rick's hand.

Standing outside, with absolutely no intention of scaring the life out of me, Rick told me about the McCulleys, Joseph in particular. He was the second sheriff of McMinn County, serving from 1842 to 1848. Back then, the sheriff not only enforced the law, but also worked as the tax collector. Since he was the first to know who had not paid their taxes and which property was to be sold at auction, quite a bit of tax property found its way into the sheriff's possession, as old deed records can attest. It seems that the office of sheriff could be quite lucrative, and McCulley amassed a notable amount of wealth. He would go on to serve on the Board of the Bank of Tennessee, and during the Civil War was a local Confederate leader, along with T. Nixon Van Dyke.

The mausoleum of McMinn County Sheriff Joseph McCulley and his wife in Athens's Cedar Grove Cemetery. *Courtesy of the McMinn County Living Heritage Museum.*

The mausoleum itself is a testament to how much money old Sheriff McCulley attained during his life. Joseph died in 1896, and his wife followed him to the grave in 1898. They were laid to rest in their crypts inside cast-iron coffins that were trimmed in silver.

Rick informed me,

> *The mausoleum was declared a safety hazard in the late 1980s, and was to be demolished. But a few of us who had an interest in preserving it got together, and organized the work to strengthen the crumbling mortar in the walls and to seal a large hole in the roof. The Heil Corporation donated the steel for the doors, and after a few months it was completed.*
>
> *We had to remove the McCulleys while the work was being done. They spent some time at McMinn Memory Gardens and at Jerry Smith Funeral home until they were returned to Cedar Grove.*

Rick told of how the coffins were built with glass viewing ports, and how the McCulleys' remains were quite well preserved after almost a hundred years; he described them as looking like the "dried apple people you can buy in Gatlinburg." They were brought back to their mausoleum in hearses provided by Jerry Smith Funeral Home, and a small reinterment ceremony was held with retired United Methodist Minister Irving Farmer officiating.

According to Rick, the McCulleys are the only people buried in Cedar Grove whose bodies have been removed and returned, and who have been taken to their graves in both horse-drawn and modern hearses. I thought about this as I stepped back outside into the sunshine and Rick locked the mausoleum's steel door. Sunlight is one of those good things in life that we take for granted. One has a greater appreciation of sunshine after spending a few minutes inside a mausoleum with two dead people, I can tell you.

Considering Sheriff McCulley's interest in providing a status symbol for himself in death, I could almost imagine a wry smile creasing his dead lips as he enjoyed the ride back to his crypt in Jerry Smith's shiny hearse, as he was a man who seems to have enjoyed the good things, in death as he did in life.

THE MURDER OF MRS. CREECH

What happened in Etowah that day horrified area residents, and to this day the act remains largely unexplained. Mrs. Annie Brock Creech was the wife of sixty-five-year-old Dr. R.C. Creech, a longtime druggist who owned a store on Tennessee Avenue in Etowah. It was the evening of

June 4, 1930, and fifty-seven-year-old Mrs. Creech was standing at the cash register near the front of her husband's store, along with their five-year-old granddaughter. Without warning, Dr. Creech approached his wife and pointed a shotgun at her from twelve feet away. The shot killed Mrs. Creech instantly and shattered the plate-glass window behind her. Arthur "Eye-dod" Blair, Etowah chief of police, and McMinn County Sheriff D.C. Duggan were notified immediately.

Dr. Creech was soon taken into custody by Sheriff Duggan at the home of his son-in-law, where he was found lying in the yard. The only statements he made were, "I had to do it," and, "She drove me to it." He stated that he had ingested strychnine in an attempt to end his own life, but no evidence of the poison was evident when Creech was examined by a doctor. Creech remained tight-lipped about the murder, saying only that he and his wife had been having marital difficulties, and that "it was an accident. I simply meant to bluff her and missed my aim." Others said he was simply "crazed by drink and had no idea of what he was doing."

In the McMinn County Jail, Creech entered into a dark stupor as he was held without bail while his sons and daughter buried their mother. Questions abounded as to why the doctor had committed such a terrible murder, and speculation only increased due to Creech's behavior in his jail cell.

He began to speak incoherently, and then he refused to eat anything except a cup of coffee in the mornings. Some wondered if he had gone insane, so a team of doctors was assembled to examine him to see if he was fit to stand trial. In front of a packed courtroom in Athens, Dr. R.A. Brock, Dr. E.C. Kensinger and Dr. C.O. Foree testified before Judge John J. Blair that they found Creech abnormal and incapable of advising his attorneys to his defense. Creech simply sat with his head in his hands throughout the proceedings, seemingly oblivious to his defense attorney, E.B. Madison. But the jury who heard the three doctors did not agree, and found Creech sane enough to be tried for the murder. Judge Blair set the trial for December 29.

While awaiting his murder trial, Dr. Creech began accepting solid food and appeared to improve in both health and mental capacity. It was election year that fall, and Bowling Shoemaker was elected to replace D.C. Duggan. Sheriff Shoemaker's brother, Mark, was appointed jailer and one of the inmates he looked after was of course Dr. Creech.

In September, Dr. Creech was in the cell that he shared with David and Arlie Casteel, Charles Voiles, Sam Perry, two Shepherd brothers, Spencer Coffman, Frank Daws and Albert Matlock. The Casteels and Shepherds, along with Voiles, Perry, Coffman and Creech, were all white men. Daws and Matlock were black, and Albert Matlock was described as a big, strong man. Just after 6:00 p.m. that September night, Matlock

In this photograph of a moonshine still bust, Jailer Mark Shoemaker is front left. Sheriff Bowling Shoemaker is third from left. *Courtesy of Ozelle Shoemaker Powers.*

called for Jailer Mark Shoemaker to bring him a bundle of clothes. When Shoemaker opened the cell door, Matlock overpowered him. In moments all the prisoners had escaped into the night, headed west from the old jail on White Street toward what is today Athens Regional Medical Center.

With the accused murderer Creech on the run, Sheriff Shoemaker organized a group of deputies and began to comb the county. Area counties were also notified of the escape. In a few days, several of the prisoners had been captured in Nonaburg, Athens, Etowah and Claxton. Eventually, Coffman and Matlock were brought in, but there was no sign of Dr. Creech.

In fact, Dr. Creech was never heard of or seen again. Rumors would abound that he had left the country and had taken up residence in Germany, but no one knows for sure, even today. It is just as likely that Creech stayed in the area of McMinn County, living out the last of his life as a man wanted for murder, dying quietly as McMinn County's most wanted fugitive that was never captured.

SALIBA SANATORIUM

To think that Athens ever had a Syrian-born doctor in 1908, and that he operated a large sanatorium near downtown Athens on the present site of All-Star Sporting Goods, might today seem a little, well, crazy.

But in fact, it is true. J.A. Saliba was born and raised in Syria, attending the American University of Beirut. He traveled over Europe and eventually came to the United States. He entered medical school at St. Louis University and then studied at the University of Tennessee Medical Department in Nashville, Birmingham Medical College and the Atlanta School of Medicine.

Saliba also studied pharmacy and held certifications in chemistry, electro-dermatology, electrophysics, electrophysiology and therapeutics, as well as specialized training in the study of the eye, ear, nose and throat. To complete his many talents, he was a surgeon as well.

He came to Athens in 1908 and established his sanatorium in a large Georgian mansion that once stood just off White Street, one block from Courthouse Square, where the old Hammer-Johnson/All-Star Sports building is located today. The huge two-story house had a massive four-columned portico and four large chimneys at each corner, tall multipaned windows and an arched doorway. Photographs of the structure show that it belonged more in Charleston, Savannah or New Orleans, rather than in Athens. It had been built around 1840 by Cleage and Crutchfield, and had once been the home of Victor Moreau Campbell and later Thomas Cleage. For several years it was also the location of the Athens branch of the Bank of Tennessee.

Based upon his education and flowing newspaper reports, it seems there was very little Dr. Saliba could not do. One account tells that he had "built up a large practice in this section and is widely and favorably known for his progressive and modern methods in the practice of his chosen profession." He was also, by all accounts, an extremely handsome man, with dark features and a thick moustache. His picture reminds one of the dapper Wyatt Earp.

Saliba's sanatorium was actually what we would describe today as a "clinic." There does not seem to be any indication of a connection with mental health as far as Saliba goes, either in practice or education. "Sanatorium" is another name for a hospital, clinic, health resort or infirmary where treatment was given for long-term illnesses.

But mental health was a concern, although its causes were sometimes explained in strange ways. For example, one East Tennessee doctor blamed all mental health problems on technology. In the early twentieth century, life

The Saliba Sanatorium occupied this mansion on White Street. *Courtesy of the McMinn County Living Heritage Museum.*

was changing fast in the economic boom of the 1920s. While we consider such growth to be a positive aspect of those times, for some it was a cause of concern.

In a short article in a 1930 *Etowah Enterprise*, it was noted that the Eastern States Hospital for the Insane in Knoxville had experienced a significant rise in patients. In the ten years prior, the hospital had seen its number of patients rise from 806 to 1,246. But according to Dr. R.E.L. Smith, the increase was easily explained: "The increase can be attributed to two factors, as I see it," said Dr. Smith, "in this gasoline age, many persons cannot adjust themselves to the rapid and constant changes. Life is too fast for them."

THE AXE UNDER THE CHURCH

John Gouldy was elected McMinn County sheriff on Friday, February 29, 1856, but his election celebration was short lived. His first day on the job was one he would not likely ever forget. The short *Athens Post* headlines of "Foul Murder!" that ran one week later spoke volumes about that Friday night, and set in motion a criminal case that even today has many unanswered questions.

The initial facts were clear enough: William Rowland was the owner of a small store in the Double Spring Community, and had been found murdered in his storeroom on Saturday morning, March 1. Evidence suggested that Rowland had been murdered with an axe, and it appeared that he had let the murderer inside under the pretext of making a purchase. It was believed that robbery was the motive, as $125 were missing from Rowland's store.

The following Monday, Sheriff Gouldy had named a suspect: a slave described as a "negro man named Jack" who belonged to O.P. Hall. Jack was arrested on suspicion of the crime, interviewed and then released.

A little over a month later, on April 18, the *Post* ran another story on the murder. It seemed that more evidence had come to light that implicated "Negro Jack," but there was a twist: Mr. Hall had taken Jack to Columbus, Georgia, and sold him to a trader, who then sold Jack to a slave owner in Macon County, about forty miles below Auburn, Alabama. The evidence against Jack must have been strong, as the county court appropriated money to buy the slave back. Colonel W.S. Calloway and Colonel Joseph McCulley (a former sheriff himself) went to Alabama and brought back "Negro Jack." The trip on horseback took several days, and one can imagine the tense situation of McCulley and Calloway camping through the dark night with the accused murderer bound near their fire, wondering what had made the man commit such a heinous crime.

A murder mystery faced McMinn County Sheriff John Gouldy on his first day in office in 1856. Years later, he would serve as a captain in the Confederate army before returning to a second term as sheriff in 1869. *Author's collection.*

The trial commenced upon Jack's return to Athens, and almost immediately Jack made a confession to the crime and implicated a white man named William Williams. Williams was also arrested, adding even more intrigue to the proceedings. The newspaper described Williams as " a native of North Carolina" who "has lived in East Tennessee for some time and possesses little sense of intelligence."

The trial lasted only two days when the jury found Jack guilty of murder and sentenced him to be hanged on June 20. But again Jack changed his story. He contradicted his former statement, and now said that Williams had no part in the murder. Jack said that Williams had told him and another slave that if they would get together enough money, Williams would take them to a free state above the Ohio River.

Jack said that he had been at Rowland's store earlier that day, and later had resolved to murder him. He returned to Rowland's store that night, and as Rowland bent down to retrieve some merchandise, Jack struck him with an axe he was carrying. He then took the money and left, hiding the murder weapon underneath the floor of Double Springs Church. With Jack's new confession, Williams was released, but there were some who were still suspicious of Williams's involvement.

The fateful day finally arrived for Jack, and the newspaper records that four to seven thousand people stood in the hot June sun to witness his execution on the gallows built downtown near the courthouse. Jack maintained his own guilt to the very end. The *Athens Post* recorded that "he mounted the gallows without any evidence of trepidation, and during the preparations for his execution showed no signs of alarm or fear."

Looking back over a century and a half since the crime, many questions remain unanswered: Was Jack indeed guilty, or was it simply a case of a slave being railroaded into a confession? Why did Jack's owner, O.P. Hall, act so quickly to sell him to an out-of-state location? Why did Jack's story change so many times? And what was the evidence that caused Jack to be brought back to McMinn County?

Whatever truth may have been is now lost to history, but local residents and Rowland descendants still speak of the horrible murder in the Double Springs Community. Another fiber of hidden history remains to produce legends and tales of a crime committed so long ago, but recalled still so many years after.

Chapter 5

PEOPLE, PLACES AND HAPPENINGS

McMinn County is made up of people and places, and history records the actions and locations that make our past come alive in these stories of rural life and rural people.

THE LAST HANGING

Sheriff William G. "Bill" Shoemaker must have looked out with disdain at the crowd of spectators gathering around the old jail on White Street on that cold morning of November 26, 1908. They had come from all parts of the county, curious of what was about to take place. On the south side of the jail was an enclosed yard surrounded by an eighteen-foot-tall fence of rough lumber, and inside the yard was the object of the crowd's attention: a gallows built for the sole purpose of hanging an accused murderer. At the thought, Shoemaker may have shook troubling thoughts from his head, for it had been almost a year since the story began.

The previous December, in a destitute house in a bad part of town, several men were engaged in a dice game of "shooting craps." Those present were Elisha Hicks, a white man, along with Beulah McGhee, Dave Sherman and Bob Henderson, who were all black. As McGhee would later claim, the men were all drunk on "mean whiskey" when a fight broke out. Hicks pulled a knife, but McGhee drew a pistol and shot Hicks. In an effort to hide the crime, McGhee and Henderson carried Hicks's body to the railroad track, hoping to cast the death as an accident. But the crime was discovered, and all three men were arrested and sentenced to hang.

Several whites argued for the sentence to be commuted, believing McGhee had acted in self defense. But in October the Tennessee Supreme Court confirmed the sentence, and Governor Patterson refused to grant respite. To the disappointment of many, including Sheriff Shoemaker,

McMinn County Sheriff William Grant Shoemaker oversaw the last public hanging that took place in McMinn County: that of Beulah McGhee, convicted of the murder of Elisha Hicks in 1908. *Author's collection.*

McGhee would hang. Contributing even more to sympathy for McGhee was what happened the morning of the execution.

Another prisoner in the McMinn County Jail was a man named Calhoun, who had been visited by his wife two weeks before McGhee's scheduled execution. When Jailer Ross Bridges brought McGhee a new suit to wear at his hanging, McGhee handed him a handwritten note that said, "Mr. Ross, if you will look over the door of Calhoun's cell you will find a saw. It has been there for two weeks. I don't know whose it is."

Bridges immediately searched Calhoun's cell, finding the saw, as well as a homemade club hidden in Calhoun's bed. It was clear that McGhee had stopped an escape and probably saved Bridges's life.

At 10:00 a.m. on the morning of his hanging, McGhee, dressed in the new black suit, stepped onto the veranda of the jail, where his picture was taken. Accompanied by Jailer Ross Bridges and some deputies, McGhee then left the north door of the jail and walked to the gallows. The only citizens allowed inside were a group of fifteen men, many of whom had tried to save McGhee from his fate. McGhee climbed the steps without assistance and stopped beside the hangman's noose, which had been borrowed from the Monroe County sheriff. Sheriff Shoemaker asked McGhee if he had any last words.

McGhee looked over to the small group of people gathered inside the yard, and then calmly said, "I am ready to die. I have no complaint to make against anybody. I thank you, Mr. Shoemaker, and your family for the kind treatment you have given me…and I want to thank you Mr. Ross. And now I am ready to die. I have repented and can meet whatever is to come." He reconfirmed his guilty plea, and then fell silent.

Bridges placed a black veil over McGhee's head, and it was only then that the condemned man displayed any kind of weakness as he said, "Mr. Ross, please hold me up." Deputy Cal Bivens secured straps around McGhee's arms and legs. Moments later, at 10:08 a.m., Sheriff Shoemaker sprang the lever. McGhee was pronounced dead at 10:25 by Dr. Shipley and Dr. Russell.

The Chattanooga newspaper reported that no member of the Elisha Hicks family came to the hanging, and that local people held a low opinion of Hicks. His twelve-year-old son was quoted as saying of him, "I have seen worse men, and then again I have seen better."

In response to the two thousand people who were still coming into Athens to see the execution, Sheriff Shoemaker reluctantly had McGhee's body placed on a cot in the jail yard and allowed the crowds to file through and view his remains. For two hours, a stream of men and women passed through. For Bill Shoemaker, the day could not have ended soon enough, and he would carry the troubling memory for the rest of his life. Years later, one of the sheriff's sisters would say, "Bill didn't want to hang that man. He didn't think he was guilty, and said that if he had been a white man he wouldn't have been hanged. It always bothered him." It was the last public hanging to take place in McMinn County.

THE WHITE STREET DITCH

The recent repaving of White Street in downtown Athens completed a several-month project to place drainage culverts under the street's west surface. Prior to the replacement, the culvert was simply a "bricked" tunnel that had very little support. A few engineers involved in the project have said that for sometime they had been a little nervous about the relatively thin layer of brick, dirt and asphalt that was holding the street up. They say they had been apprehensive every time a large truck traveled down the street.

But many years ago, before the brick culvert was put in place, a long ditch ran along the west side of White Street that was more or less an Athens landmark. I found a reference to it in a historical booklet titled "McMinn County Tennessee, 1819–1968," by Charles Keith Jr. Mr. Keith gives the following description:

> There was on the west side of White St. a large open ditch, between the walk and the street. It was about 8 feet wide and varied from 3 feet to 8 feet deep, and was walled up on both sides from Bank Street to where the Farmer's Bank is now. Bridges were from each store across to the street. The (ends of) the ditch was not walled up, and wagons would line up in the summer and sell their watermelons and other produce. In the fall and early winter this ditch would be full of wagons loaded with apples, chestnuts, scaly bark hickory nuts, cabbage, etc.

Mr. Keith, writing in the late 1960s, made reference to a description of the ditch from seventy years earlier, around the turn of the twentieth century. In those days, the courthouse and downtown area were places where people gathered and visited, especially on "court days." They were places to see the goings-on in the county and to catch up on the latest news and gossip. It would not be uncommon for a sizable crowd to gather, and this fact was not lost on the farmers who used the ditch to sell their goods. As Mr. Keith writes, "These wagons would come here for court, which usually began the second Monday in December and lasted several weeks. However, the wagons usually sold their supplies out in two weeks."

What we might consider an eyesore and an inconvenience today was accepted as not only practical but also beautiful at that time. Old photographs of downtown Athens show large trees up and down almost every street, and White Street was no exception. Mr. Keith describes, "Seventy odd years ago there was along this ditch a beautiful stand of large elm trees. These trees were all destroyed when the streets were paved…Athens was once noted for its shady trees."

Being such an active location, the ditch must surely have attracted quite a number of people who gathered to buy produce or simply to visit with each other. I am also told it was a common place for students to go when playing hooky on warm spring days. Many an angry schoolmaster must have chased his runaway students down the ditch and around the wagons in an effort to get them back to the classroom.

The ditch and the bridges that spanned it are long gone now, having been bricked and paved over in the 1930s. No wagons selling fresh produce have parked along White Street in many years, although occasionally an overalled farmer may still be seen out Decatur Pike selling tomatoes and watermelons from an old station wagon. But the story of the White Street ditch has been preserved in the writings of men like Charles Keith Jr., and copies of his booklet can still be found in the McMinn County Historical Society.

When "Whiteways" Were All the Rage

We take for granted the fine roads and highways that now grace the hills and valleys of East Tennessee. No matter if the weather is reflective of the dry summer or the cold dampness of winter, our roads allow us to travel into Virginia, Kentucky, North Carolina and Georgia in less than half a day.

Good roads are a direct reflection of the success of local government. When citizens are able to travel uninhibited to conduct business, shop, recreate or simply pay a visit, a community is able to thrive. Good roads are the veins and arteries that carry a community's lifeblood.

And so it seems strange to imagine the muddy pig trails that were the roads of East Tennessee fewer than one hundred years ago. Newspapers and personal accounts tell of bottomless mudholes that would swallow up a wagon or a Model-T Ford. Big horses were favored by the men who could afford them, like Judge Charles Fleming Keith, because the tall steeds "kept them out of the mud." Even city streets were dirt, and combined with the animal waste associated with horse-drawn wagons, hacks and buggies, they made for a messy and rather smelly downtown. This accounts for a law in Athens as late as 1922 that prohibited the

Along with roads, railroad construction played an important role in McMinn County's early development of infrastructure. This railroad crew is busy constructing a bridge along the Athens-Tellico Railroad in 1894. Note the small children working alongside the adults on the scaffolding. *Courtesy of the Englewood Textile Museum.*

hitching of animals within two blocks of the town square. By 1917, only 351 automobiles were in McMinn County.

No street or highway departments existed in the early days. In cities and towns such as Athens, the town marshal was charged with issuing summons to citizens who were assigned "road duty." Persons owning property that was adjacent to a road or street were responsible for road maintenance and upkeep. Unpaved streets were oiled in the summers to keep the dust down.

While today we can literally drive from one end of the state to the other in less than a day, a hundred years ago a simple trip from the country to the county seat was an all-day affair. It is no wonder that travel by rail was favored over any other means of transportation. Even in its early days, it was cleaner and faster than slogging through a muddy road.

And as McMinn County can claim the first railroad in Tennessee, we were also home to the first paved road in East Tennessee. In March of 1919, a meeting was held at the courthouse supporting legislative action to fund better roads. With the support of Representative Harry Burn, construction was begun in 1920 to concrete the section of Lee Highway from Athens to Calhoun, which before then had been almost impassable in an automobile. Part of this first paved road is still visible on the property now owned by Calhoun Transportation, just off Highway 11 in Calhoun. In 1924, the road was extended north out of Athens along Ingleside Avenue.

The impact of these road improvements on McMinn County was seen almost immediately. Within the space of about six years, from 1916 to 1922, Athens went from a dark, dusty, country town to a bustling modern city with "a sidewalk system, public square and streets leading to both railway stations have concrete systems...streets around the square and those leading to the railroad station are lighted with a whiteway...a drinking fountain has been installed." Athens could brag about having a "pure water supply" and "electricity furnished from a plant at Parksville" (according to the *Semi-Weekly Post* of December 1922). The *Etowah Enterprise* on September 18, 1924, carried a short article stating that "a survey of traffic over part of the Lee Highway that travels through Athens revealed 1,000 cars pass through Athens daily" and that "prior to the completion of the concrete road between Athens and Calhoun, a distance of 14 miles, cars did not exceed one hundred per day."

Today, we think little of the dirt roads and streets that our area was plagued with only a few decades ago. But when the first "whiteway" and paved street were opened in Athens in October of 1922, it received quite a bit of press and was celebrated with what was referred to as a "community carnival."

It was this time of growth after World War I that made East Tennessee what it is today. And it all started with a small stretch of muddy road in McMinn County.

THE "GREAT HAILSTONE" OF 1932

The citizens of Athens, Tennessee, headed for cover as a freak hailstorm passed through McMinn County on July 30, 1932. For several minutes, pea- and walnut-sized pellets showered the area of downtown Athens, covering the streets and dancing off rooftops and automobiles.

As the storm moved on up the valley, Athenians left the storefronts of the downtown square to investigate the weather phenomenon. Several interesting chunks of summer ice were located, but a crowd quickly gathered at the southeast corner of the square. There, in front of the Robert E. Lee Hotel, lay a ten- to twelve-pound chunk of ice.

Voices became excited. People pointed and waved others over to see the huge hailstone. "Have you ever seen anything like it?" was the common quote of the day, as was the sobering, "What if that had hit someone?"

Someone stooped down and picked up the giant hailstone, and the crowd escorted the chunk of ice into Red Chapman's Café, where it was placed into the icebox to preserve it. Throughout the day, people came in and out of Chapman's Café, anxious to view the unbelievably large hailstone. One wonders how much business this generated for Mr. Chapman. After a while, Chapman began chipping off pieces of the hailstone to cool off glasses of iced tea that he then sold to his customers. The pieces of the "Great Hailstone" must surely have tasted especially refreshing in the late July heat.

While the commotion continued, someone decided that the newspaper should be notified of this natural wonder that had fallen from the sky into downtown Athens. The call to the newspaper was made from the drugstore that was in the front portion of the Robert E. Lee Hotel and was owned by S.B. "Bullet" Boyer.

Bullet and his employee, Howard Bales, listened with interest as the call to the newspaper was placed, and nodded their heads intently as the excited citizen told the man on the other end of the line of the incident that had happened right outside their store. It was only after the citizen left that Boyer and Bales slapped each other on the back and nearly fell to the floor of the drugstore with laughter. Indeed, a giant hailstone had fallen from the sky—but not from the altitude most citizens thought.

Known for his quick sense of humor, Bullet Boyer had been watching the hailstorm outside when he suddenly had an idea. He called for Howard

Bullet Boyer's store occupied the right front of the Robert E. Lee Hotel. The giant "hailstone" was discovered on the sidewalk in front of this store. *Courtesy of the McMinn County Living Heritage Museum.*

Bales, and instructed him to fetch a large chunk of ice from the fifty-pound block in the drugstore's icebox. Bales, a bit of a prankster himself, knew just where this was going. Breaking off a large chunk, Bales tucked the ice under his coat, rode the elevator upstairs and went to a second-floor corner window. When he was sure no one was looking, he tossed the ice out into the summer storm. To the glee of both tricksters, it didn't even break when it struck the street below.

Throughout the entire affair, Boyer and Bales played dumb while the rest of Athens fell for their practical joke. A photograph of the hailstone graced the front page of the next day's local paper. The prank went over so well that they didn't say a word for the next several weeks.

According to the story of this incident recorded in *Tall Tales and Unusual Happenings in McMinn County*, neither of the men gave away their involvement while Athens and McMinn County continued to wonder about the "Great Hailstone." But the extent of their joke went far beyond the county line.

A few weeks after the hailstone had been completely chipped away to cool off Mr. Chapman's iced tea, two customers walked into Bullet Boyer's drugstore. They were two General Electric employees currently working in Athens. While visiting with the owner, the men casually mentioned to Boyer that they had recently seen a story about Athens in the *New York Times*.

"Oh, really," said Boyer casually. "What was it about?"

The men shrugged and replied, "Something about a giant hailstone."

71

JESSE'S UNCLE DANIEL

In November of 1849, an eighty-year-old man felt that the end of his days was near. On his farm on Middle Creek, about six miles east of Athens, he made out his last will and testament. A man of principle, he had lived in McMinn County for twenty-five years, and this farm was his final place of residence after many years of moving, fighting Indians and settling America's first frontier.

His name was Jesse, and he had been born to his parents, Israel and Martha, in the year 1748 in Pennsylvania. When he was still a small boy, his parents moved to Rowan County, North Carolina. During the summer of 1756, his parents died and eight-year-old Jesse, along with his brother Jonathan, went to live with his father's twenty-one-year-old brother. This uncle, Daniel, was only recently married himself, to a young woman named Rebecca.

For about ten years, the family lived on Sugar Tree Creek near present Mocksville, North Carolina. In 1766, Jesse and his brother moved with Uncle Daniel westward, to a new farm on the Yadkin River where Daniel had spent several years hunting. It was a frontier community, far removed from significant settlements, constantly under threat from Indians and outlaws. Uncle Daniel would continue his long hunting trips, once being gone for two years. When he returned with a beard and long hair, Jesse didn't even recognize him.

During his exploring, Uncle Daniel had become enamored with the distant lands in Kentucky, and in 1773 he made an attempt to move his family there. But Indians attacked part of the group, killing several young men, including Daniel's seventeen-year-old son James. Jesse and James had been raised as brothers, and the loss was devastating to the family. The entire settlement party decided to turn back, and for a while they lived on the Holston River, near present-day Kingston, Tennessee.

By then, Jesse was a grown man, and in 1774 he married Sarah McMahan and began raising his own family. Throughout the Revolutionary War, Uncle Daniel pushed farther and farther into Kentucky, establishing settlements and fighting Indians. Jesse resided for several years in Burke and Boone Counties, North Carolina, where he and Sarah raised eight children. Following the example of his Uncle Daniel, they were members of the Baptist church. In Kentucky, Uncle Daniel found himself in legal trouble over his land, and began to look for other places to settle. In 1799, several of Jesse's uncles, aunts and cousins moved to Missouri, and among them was his elderly Uncle Daniel. In 1820, Jesse received word that Uncle Daniel had passed away.

Uncle Daniel was a devoutly religious man, once writing, "For my part I am as ignorant as a Child all the Relegan I have to love and feer god believe in Jesus Christ Do all the good to my neighbors and my Self that I can and Do as Little harm as I can help and trust God's mercy for the rest and I believe god never made a man of principel to be Lost." It is recorded that he did his best to raise Jesse and Jonathan, as well as his own children he had with Rebecca.

In 1824, after a dispute over religious principles in North Carolina, Jesse purchased land in newly formed McMinn County, Tennessee. Not long afterward, he continued following the Baptist tradition as a member of Zion Hill Baptist Church. The land he bought on Middle Creek already had a cabin built on it, which Jesse expanded to accommodate his family and his female servant, Dinah. For the next twenty-five years, he lived and worked on the farm on Middle Creek. Not long after preparing his will, Jesse died in December of 1829, and was buried on the farm.

Jesse was known to many people in McMinn County, especially in his later years. He must surely have passed stories down to his children and grandchildren of his beloved uncle who had raised and cared for him. The mere mention of Jesse's name was quick to cause conversation, for his given name was Boone.

His uncle, Daniel Boone, the man who had taken him in and raised him as a child, instilling his own principles in young Jesse as he did with his own children, was of course the legendary hunter, scout, Indian fighter and father of Kentucky.

THE SCHOOL AND CHURCH THAT JAKE COOK BUILT

In May of 1870, a baby was born to George and Amelia Cook, former slaves of Judge J.B. Cooke of Athens. The baby boy was named Jacob Lincoln Cook. By 1878, both George and Amelia had died, and young Jacob, or Jake as he was called, was taken in by two other former slaves, "Uncle" Nelse and "Aunt" Hildy Gettys. The Gettyses seemed to have taken great care in allowing Jake to obtain an education.

Jake became a dedicated and accomplished student, so much that he caught the attention of a local physician, Dr. Parkinson. With Parkinson's help, Jake obtained a scholarship to Fisk University in Nashville, Tennessee. An excellent singer, Jake became a member of the famous Fisk Jubilee Singers.

After attending Fisk, Jake enrolled in Knoxville College. Jake paid his way through hard work and support from people back home in Athens, both black and white. After his graduation in 1888, he entered Allegheny Theological Seminary in Pittsburgh, Pennsylvania, intent on becoming a Presbyterian minister. In April of 1890, he obtained his license as a minister and returned to Athens, where he established a Presbyterian mission in a building occasionally used as a dance hall. After two years of work, Jake founded the First United Presbyterian Church in a newly constructed building on Jackson Street, on the dance hall property owned by Uncle Nelse Gettys. In *The History of First United Presbyterian Church, Athens, TN*, it is recorded that "the Reverend J.L. Cook, a forceful and eloquent speaker, attracted many of the young people from the other churches, and many of them joined, forming the first congregation." Jake continued for several years as its minister.

Having reaped the benefits of his own education, Jake, along with the assistance of the Presbyterian church, organized a small, three-room school called the Academy of Athens, located near the Southern Depot on the hill above the town. According to the website of Jake's grandson, Jean Lawrence Cook, MD, most black schools in Tennessee at that time were one-room schools with only one teacher. The Athens Academy was certainly an exception.

By that time, Jake's first wife, Pocahontas Gibson, had died. He then married Zella Cornelia Lawrence in 1898, a pretty young woman he had met in Boston. She would give Jake a son, and she also cared for the daughter from his previous marriage as if she were her own.

Jake remained at Athens Academy until the summer of 1900, when he was appointed the first black president of Henderson Normal Institute in North Carolina. Zella died shortly afterward from typhoid fever in 1900, leaving Jake twice widowed with two young children. After a short while, he married a young woman named Amelia. But again, the marriage would be cut short by death when Amelia died in childbirth on February 9, 1903. Now thrice widowed, and at only thirty-three years old, Jake's remarkable life ended when he died on July 5 of the same year. He was brought back and buried at Cedar Grove Cemetery beside Amelia.

In 1925, twenty-two years after Jake's death, the Athens Academy was destroyed by fire. The school continued to be held in the United Presbyterian Church, but a desire remained to build a new school to continue the educational tradition begun by Jake Cook. With funding from McMinn County, the City of Athens and the Rosenwald Fund, a new all-black public school was built and opened December 10, 1926. Known as J.L. Cook School, the building had six classrooms, an auditorium and six teachers, including the principal, W.E. Nash. There were 150 pupils enrolled. As it grew in both reputation and enrollment, the school was enlarged to two stories and became the J.L. Cook High School, known throughout the state and the South as one of the premier black schools. It continued as such for several decades until the desegregation movement in the 1960s, when J.L. Cook High School was a victim of the movement's good intentions. While the black community supported continuing the Cook School, the local education officials felt that an all-black school was no longer needed in McMinn County. So J.L. Cook High School was closed forever in 1966.

J.L. Cook High School is gone, but Jake's legacy is remembered in the park where the school once stood, as well as in the Presbyterian church building that still stands as a landmark in Athens. Cook School alumni are spread throughout the South today. With their basic education obtained within the halls of Cook School, they continue the work of its founder, a man who through education and a care for his fellow men rose above his humble roots, born in a community with strong ties between its people, regardless of race.

FREE HILL: A FORGOTTEN COMMUNITY

For some it was an eyesore, a ghetto that was nothing more than a nuisance to the growing city of Athens. To others, it was a symbol of pride, though tarnished and in need of repair. It had been, over one hundred years earlier, a community of free blacks that once overlooked the town of Athens from a high hill to the north. It was known by its inhabitants as Free Hill.

Free Hill, established some time prior to the Civil War, was occupied and owned by black Americans who, unlike many of their brethren at the time, were not slaves. These free men not only owned their own homes and land, but many were also skilled tradesmen or owned their own businesses. Two prominent blacks in the area were William Heyward Ferguson, an educated minister, and Robert "Bob" McGaughey, a skilled tinworker whose shop was downtown where the old First National Bank/Johnson Building is now located.

It appears that it was not an uncommon thing for blacks to own businesses in Athens in those days prior to the Civil War. An advertisement in the June 2, 1854 *Athens Post* refers to "Bath Houses" operated by Clint Cleage and Nelson Gettys, "two enterprising men from Africa." In the early twentieth century, Albert Evans owned and operated a successful barbershop at 8 North White Street that was even listed in the 1916 Athens Telephone Directory. Mr. Evans ran a good business and lived in a fine home, although he could not cut his own people's hair. For in the days of Jim Crow laws, no white patron would sit in the same barber chair that had been used by a black patron.

The community of Free Hill was centered on St. Mark's Methodist Church, founded in 1865 and built on land obtained in 1867. It was the first church in McMinn County that was founded by and for blacks. A black school, which some refer to as the first in Athens, was operated on Free Hill under the direction of William Ferguson, and later by his son Arthur. The school was located near the present fellowship hall of St. Mark's, and it was in this school that the members of St. Mark's worshipped until a proper church building was completed several years later. William published assorted periodicals after 1891 that molded a positive public opinion toward the African Methodist Episcopal Church, and also contributed to the establishment of Greene County High School. Arthur Ferguson, following his father's example, obtained his education from Livingston College and was instrumental in the founding of Cook School in Athens. Also a skilled woodworker, Arthur Ferguson and his seven sons are credited with building the original foundation of St. Mark's Methodist, which was completed in 1882 by John McDonald. Ferguson also operated a coal yard, and was the first black shipping clerk at the Athens Woolen Mill. For many in Athens's black community, Free Hill was symbolic as a community that had "made it on its own."

But over time, the land changed hands and much of Free Hill fell into disrepair and neglect. When urban renewal targeted Free Hill in the early 1960s, the property in the area was bought up in its entirety. Some say that false promises were made to its inhabitants that the community would be demolished and reconstructed on the same site, and would be available for resale to its inhabitants. If there were any promises, it is clear they were never fulfilled. For the most part, Free Hill had completely disappeared by the mid-1970s. The area is now most noted for the YMCA, the Athens Municipal Building and a college soccer field.

No marker commemorates Athens's pre–Civil War community of free blacks, and little writing has been done to preserve the fact that it ever existed. Only St. Mark's stands on its original location, marking the site of Free Hill, a community that once overlooked Athens, but now lives only in the dimming memories of its residents.

I am indebted to the writings of Ms. Augusta Witt in *McMinn County: A History of Its People*, Ms. Lee Cates and Mr. Wally Ferguson in obtaining this information.

When the Light Shone on Ridge Road

In eastern McMinn County, there is what remains of a once well-used wagon road that follows the Liberty Hill ridges. Parts of this old road are

Old Liberty Hill Church of Christ, pictured in 1890. The church used as a Civil War pest house sat to the rear of this building. *Author's collection.*

still visible between the Coltharp Community in Monroe County and the Liberty Hill Community in McMinn County. Old records call this trace the Old Ridge Road, and on a lonely hilltop along this old path, covered in forest and far removed from the nearest modern road, a few stones mark the site of one of the area's earliest churches and cemeteries, known as the Ridge Road Church.

The present Liberty Hill Church of Christ proudly traces its roots back to this original place of worship, where several present members are descendants of the Casses, Burgers, Daughertys, Casteels and Wades that worshiped at Ridge Road in the 1820s. Some other church sites in the area are also as old, all having been organized just after the Hiwassee Purchase in 1819: Big Springs Baptist Church of Christ (1822), Calhoun Methodist (1823), Eastanaulee Baptist (1819), Union McMinn near Niota (1825) and Zion Hill near present Englewood (1822). By 1824, Baptist and Methodist churches were also in Athens.

But the Ridge Road Church stands out, especially when one visits the site today. Of some fifty or more graves, only three or four can still be found. Nothing remains of the log church that sat just south of the cemetery. Standing there, on that lonely wooded hillside, it is easy to imagine the people who came to this area to find little more than the same forests and rugged hills. The area was less than friendly in those early days of settlement. The roads were little more than game trails, winding across steep hillsides and through dense forest that limited visibility to only a few yards. Land grants and property claims often overlapped, which resulted in settlers traveling over a dangerous route to find that their plot of land existed only on paper, and they had come for nothing. Others who did manage to secure a hill or hollow for themselves could look forward to nothing but backbreaking labor in clearing the land for a small farm. The husband, wife and children would all have to work from daylight until dark, sleeping in a rude brush-covered shelter until the crop was planted, and only then could their attention be turned to the felling of trees for a rude cabin home. Throughout all of this, the family would live under the threat of not only the wind and wildlife, but also of roaming thieves and bushwhackers, both Indian and white, who would prey on any man they found alone. Often, there would be no neighbors close by; perhaps the nearest would be over the far ridge, an hour's trek on horseback.

With all this in mind, it is interesting to note that these people would take the time out of their already busy and difficult lives to build a place of worship like Ridge Road. Perhaps even before some had built their own houses, they would devote their energies into building their church.

The building of the church was surely a welcome time for all, some community fellowship in a lonely new area, all the men laying their hands together to set the freshly hewn logs, the women cooking a meal over a nearby fire, children playing while the work was being done. They would have talked of their travel to their new lands, what work they'd gotten done, what plans they had to build new lives and new farms. Later would come the creek dams and millraces to grind the corn. First they would build their church.

Imagine those Sundays, coming together in rain, heat, sleet and snow after a rough wagon or horseback ride, finding the welcome shelter of their log church. They would have sung songs we would still recognize today: "Amazing Grace," "We're Marching to Zion," "On Jordan's Stormy Banks." There would be no instrumental music. Barney Casteel would stand on the puncheon floor and preach the Gospel, they would observe the Lord's Communion and after a few more songs the congregants would shake hands and visit with each other, learn about how the neighbor across the ridge was faring or about the new family that had just arrived down the hollow.

With all the dangers and pitfalls of building new homes and communities, the importance of building those first churches is clear. The people who built the Ridge Road Church had little to fear in the present world, so long as they organized themselves as the worn Bibles under their arms told them to do. And the building would serve not only as a place of worship, but also as a center point and birthplace of the community. When the first of their members passed away, they interred them in the rich ground within sight of the church door. With every Sunday visit, they would not be forgotten there.

As needs changed and the community grew, the congregation would eventually leave the Ridge Road site in 1840 for Liberty Hill two miles away, where a store and a mill would be built. The old church would disappear, as would most of the gravestones. But to forget those early people would be to forget what was important to them, knowing where they would be just after the sun rose each Sunday morning, putting away the work and trouble for just one day, riding in the swaying wagon toward Ridge Road.

The Old Liberty Hill School, which sat across the road from the present Liberty Hill Church of Christ, was an important part of that rural community. *Courtesy of the McMinn County Living Heritage Museum.*

McMINN COUNTY'S "BAND OF BROTHERS"

The nation was stunned when newspapers and radio stations announced the deaths of the Sullivan brothers on November 13, 1942. The five brothers, all from Waterloo, Iowa, made headlines early in World War II when they volunteered for service to avenge the death of their friend Bill Ball on the USS *Arizona* at Pearl Harbor. But their ship, the USS *Juneau*, was torpedoed less than a year later in November 1942, and all five of the Sullivans perished, along with some seven hundred of their fellow crewmen.

The Sullivan brothers were better known than most, but there were many families nationwide who went to World War II together. Even in McMinn County, several families provided sons to go to war. One of these was the Sims family of Athens.

Elbert and Essie Sims lived off Old Highway 11, and had raised a large family of ten children. There were six sisters and four sons: William, Marlin, Sam and Paul. By the time World War II began, the oldest of the Sims boys, William, was already in the navy, having enlisted in 1938. William was involved in the development of a new diving bell, and he was on a crew that participated in the rescue of the crew of the downed submarine *Squalus* off the East Coast in 1939. After Pearl Harbor, William was followed

79

into the navy in 1942 by Sam, and in 1943 Marlin volunteered rather than wait to be drafted. All three of these Sims brothers served in the Pacific theater: William on a submarine, Sam as a machinist and Marlin on a minesweeper.

Only Paul, the youngest, remained at home. When he turned seventeen in 1944, he persuaded his father to accompany him to Nashville so that he could follow his brothers and enlist in the navy. Elbert signed for his youngest son and returned home. That night, he told his wife, "You know, those boys over there tried to get me to enlist in the navy." Essie replied, "Well, you might as well go on. You won't be any good to me moping around here." Elbert, a World War I veteran himself, went back to the recruiter the next day, reportedly saying, "If you're going to take all my boys, you might as well take me too."

While Paul followed his brothers to the Pacific theater, their father was sent to the Atlantic, where he took part in the landings on the Normandy coast as a gunner's mate. A concussion wound he received in action would plague him the rest of his life.

The Sullivan tragedy caused the navy to discourage family members from serving on the same ship, unless the siblings signed a waiver of request to do so. Today, according to Naval Military Press Command, siblings may not serve on the same ship if the ship is in a "hostile force area."

Unlike the Sullivans, all but one of the Sims brothers survived their wartime service. At the request of his parents, Paul lies buried in the Galapagos Islands, where he was killed in a plane crash in May of 1945 while scouting for submarines as an aviation gunner's mate.

As the members of the 278th Armored Cavalry Regiment are now participating in their pre-deployment training, it is interesting to consider other families from our area who have allowed their fathers, sons and brothers to serve our country in times of war. We keep the 278th in our prayers, as they follow the example of volunteers like the Sullivans and Simses.

Over the passage of time, Elbert, William, Marlin and Sam Sims have passed away. No brother remains to tell the story of the Sims family and this "band of brothers" from McMinn County.

NAMES OF WHITE ON A SEA OF BLUE

Hanging in the wall of the City Recorder's Office in Niota is a six- by six-foot handmade quilt. It is constructed of a simple design, made of thirty-six sky blue squares that hold identical white-stitched circles. Each circle is divided into nine equal sections radiating from a circle in the middle. Around the center circle of each square reads "Niota PTA—1928."

The quilt was a fundraiser project by the 1928 Niota PTA, and like the quilt itself, its design was of a simple plan. Each circle was sewn independently, with the name of the person constructing the section sewn inside. Each of the nine radiating sections was sold to others in the community, who could have their names sewn in at the cost of one dollar per section. Once the quilt was completed, it was auctioned off for an additional sum to Mr. C.L. Knox, who gave it to his daughter, Ora, who had sewn one of the circles. Ora later married and moved to California.

Years passed, and Ora contacted her brother Noel, who had remained in Niota. She told Noel the blanket didn't mean anything in California. It needed to be in Niota, she said. So about ten years ago, Ora Knox Stevenson sent the quilt back to its original home.

Noel recently introduced me to the quilt and the stories behind it. It has been well cared for over the years; its writing is still a bright white, the circles cast over the blue background like clouds in the sky. The names contained in each center circle and its nine sections are a record of history, a literal who's who in 1928 Niota.

"There is the circle done by Mrs. Febb Burn," said Noel, his aged fingers drifting over the glass that protects the quilt. "And around her name are the initials of all her children." Ms. Burn was the mother of state legislator Harry T. Burn, who had cast the deciding vote on the Nineteenth Amendment just eight years before the creation of the quilt. Hers is the only circle that utilizes initials rather than names.

"A lot of people in here. There's the circle sewn by Mrs. John I. Forrest, and there's the one by Mrs. Joe McGahey, a local doctor. And there is Ms. Myrtle Webb, an area home improvement agent back then." Many other names also appear: Willson, Forrest, Staley, Collins, Shoemaker, Cate, Snyder. A few names appear more than once, in different sections of different circles. Noel explained, "You could have your name put in as many sections as you wanted to buy. Only the people with names in the sections had to pay. The lady who sewed the circle could have her name in the middle for free."

While the design is the same for each section, the stitching is unique to each person who did the sewing. Some of the names are stitched in single lines, while others are boldly displayed with double lines. Some are printed, and others sewn in flowing, cursive letters.

"This was my family's section," Noel told me, pointing to the circle with Ora Knox's name in the center. "Ora was fourteen when she sewed it."

The nine sections around Ora's name contain those of Noel, Jake, Horace, Glenn, Ara and Noel's parents, C.L. and Mrs. C.L. Knox. The two sections on top hold the names of Mr. and Mrs. J.M. Wattenbarger.

"My mother's parents," said Noel. "My grandmother Wattenbarger was a Dodson, and her father had fought in the Civil War. I can remember him as an old man living in Englewood."

Noel pointed to another name on the quilt, that of Joy Staley. "Joy wasn't born until 1929," he said wryly. "But they were able to squeeze her into Mrs. J.S. Lewis's section because it was late getting finished. We still laugh about how she managed to get in there."

Looking over the names of the supporters of the Niota PTA, I was impressed with the amount of community support and the creative fundraising going on in 1928. I wonder if those people who purchased sections or sewed the names of the quilt realized at the time how they were recording the history of their community.

By my calculations, thirty-six circles with nine one-dollar sections each must have raised about $324 for the PTA. Noel could not remember how much his father had bid on the quilt in the auction seventy-six years ago; not that the amount really matters.

What was a simple fundraiser in 1928 is today a treasure worth more to Niota and McMinn County than could ever be measured.

ENGLEWOOD'S STARLIGHT MOVIE THEATER

On a warm summer evening in 1925, a group of people gathered in downtown Englewood. In a lot bordered by the rear of Main Street's buildings, across the street from a small hotel near the Chestnut house, the crowd stood and talked with anticipation. All ages of people were there, as well as a mix of a few wealthy business owners, several middle-class millworkers and some poor farmers. They must have visited and spoken to each other of crops, gossip and local politics, and they could not help but watch some men working diligently on the side of the building in front of them. After several minutes, the men completed their work in hanging a large, white sheet of cloth to the brick wall. Evening had grown darker with the setting sun, and soon a light came on in a box to the rear of the crowd, and with that all suddenly fell silent. On the large cloth sheet danced moving pictures. There were no sounds as the actors moved through the story. Occasionally the crowd would laugh or murmur at the words that appeared on the screen between the silent scenes, but for the most part they simply stood still and quiet, watching the movie in the cool darkness.

In the days when a trip to another town took most of the day in a wagon or a puttering Model-T over a rutted, curving road, small towns like Englewood ran thriving businesses to entertain their residents. Black-and-white silent movies were shown for a few cents per head outdoors when the weather was good. A skating rink once occupied the upstairs of one of Englewood's Main Street buildings. Etowah once had a bowling alley upstairs in a building at the corner of Eighth Street and Tennessee Avenue. And of course the Strand Theater always drew crowds from the Englewood-Etowah area for movies and shows.

Athens had two theaters around the turn of the century, even before the old Strand Theater that was completed around 1935. The Dixie Theater was in the present MouseWorks location on North Jackson Street, behind the old Annex Hotel. There was also the Picto Theater at 20 South Jackson, near the present Athens Supply property. I am told of Athens's first pizza parlor, which was across North Jackson, upstairs in the building beside Mars Hill Church. Later on the Midway Drive-In was one of many outdoor movie venues in the state.

Today, little consideration is given to an evening trip to Chattanooga or Knoxville to catch a movie, go ice skating, have a nice meal and still make it home before midnight. With improvements to roads and automobiles, as well as the construction of interstate freeways in the late 1960s and early 1970s, people were no longer limited to their small towns. It was a double-edged sword: more opportunities for citizens drew them out of their hometowns, but the hometowns began to shrivel and die. Today, the skating rinks and bowling alleys have disappeared from the small downtowns of Etowah and Englewood, having been relegated to light show arcades and multi-entertainment complexes. No theaters have been in downtown Athens since the mid-1970s, and even the Midway Drive-In, although still a quality operation, is one of the last of its kind.

Downtowns now rely more on beauty and quality of life than bowling and skating. Small restaurants, antique stores, coffee houses and tours of historic sites, accompanied with pleasant atmospheres, clean streets, interesting architecture and renovated buildings, are now the driving forces that make downtowns attractive places to work, shop and relax. It is a challenge to compete with the metropolitan areas, but downtowns have discovered that small-town atmospheres and values can't be reproduced anywhere else. Property owners, downtown organizations and citizens are learning to work together to look back to the past, developing what resources they have now to plan for a better future.

And who knows? Maybe a new crowd will gather on a summer night in Englewood again, to talk of politics and gardens and enjoy an outdoor movie screening on the side of a sheet-covered building.

Downtown Englewood, around the turn of the twentieth century. Until the first indoor theater was built in the 1940s, movies were shown on the side of a building outdoors. *Courtesy of the Englewood Textile Museum.*

THE SUFFRAGIST

In the summer of 2004, delegates arrived in New York City for the Republican National Convention, to officially name George W. Bush as the Republican candidate for president. One hundred years ago that year, the Republican Convention was held in Chicago on June 21–23, 1904.

Theodore Roosevelt was the sitting president at the time, having been sworn in at a home in Buffalo, New York, following the assassination of President McKinley three years earlier. Roosevelt, widely admired for his colorful and courageous character, was the controlling force throughout the convention, and was confident of winning his party's nomination, which of course he did. The Republican went on that year to win election to a second term.

Much like today, international and domestic affairs took center stage at the Republican Convention, but one issue was gaining prominence throughout the country: voting rights for women. It is interesting to note that four women arrived at the convention as delegates—a first—but no plank for women's suffrage was added to the party platform.

One of the four women delegates to the 1904 convention was Mrs. Susan West from Idaho, and she was no stranger to such an event. Four years earlier, she had attended the 1900 Republican National Convention in Philadelphia and had supported the nomination of the late President McKinley. In fact, Mrs. West's presence at the 1900 convention made her the first woman in history to attend a national convention as a delegate. Women in Idaho had obtained the right to vote in 1896, but still there was no amendment to the U.S. Constitution. In this light, Mrs. West was indeed making history.

During a recent conference in Buffalo, New York, my good friend Circuit Judge Carroll Ross was touring the home where President Teddy Roosevelt was sworn into office in 1901, following the death of President McKinley. On one of the displays was the picture of Mrs. Susan West, and Judge Ross was kind enough to share with me a discovery he had made. For underneath Mrs. West's picture was the following information, taken from an article in the *Buffalo Evening News*, June 23, 1904:

> *Mrs. J.B. (Susan) west of Lewiston, Idaho, is the only woman delegate to the national Republican Convention. This is the second time she has had that honor bestowed upon her. She is a native of Cog Hill, McMinn County, Tennessee, and her maiden name was Susan M. Henderson. At the age of 19 she was graduated from the Grant Memorial University at Athens. She and her husband went to Idaho in 1891. She has since been interested in the politics of the State, in which women are allowed to vote, and stands high in the councils of her party. Coupled with a most pleasing personality, she has a lot of common sense ideas about the possibilities of her sex, decidedly at variance with the crank notions of so many of the women suffragists. She is one of the brightest women in the great Northwest, and is held in high esteem by the best men and women in Idaho.*

Lenora Henson, curator of the Theodore Roosevelt Inaugural National Historic Site, has provided me with what information she has gathered on Susan West, giving me and Judge Ross a bit of hidden history to investigate. McMinn County is widely known for Harry T. Burn's 1919 vote that provided passage of the Nineteenth Amendment after receiving a letter from his mother in Niota. But it seems that a native McMinn County woman was working toward national suffrage twenty years before Burn's vote. Evidently, McMinn County and Tennessee have not one, but two ties to national women's suffrage.

Susan West's life and her roots in McMinn County will require further study. To quote Ms. Henson, "When I found her information, I was immediately taken with her." I'll be interested to see what other accomplishments were performed by the first woman delegate to the

National Republican Convention, and who should also be "held in high esteem" in her native county.

THE FISHER TYPEWRITER

It was a grand financial venture that took place in 1887 when the Athens Mining and Manufacturing Company was chartered in the North Athens area. North Athens was planned to be a modern city, with Woodward Avenue as its main street that would overshadow the old courthouse area. Stock was sold off to build a grand hotel, a school, a railroad depot, assorted manufacturing mills and homes. The original charter was signed by many influential men of the time, including Robert J. Fisher. But by 1889, the corporation had quickly fallen on hard times, and was soon disbanded. But that is a story for another day.

At the moment I am typing this article on my computer, I cannot help but think of Robert J. Fisher. You see, Mr. Fisher was many things: he established Athens's first hosiery mill, he brought the first known bicycle into town and he is believed to be the first McMinn Countian to ride in an airplane. Back at the turn of the twentieth century, those were notable accomplishments. But Fisher was also an inventor, and he brought quite a bit of national fame to his hometown in East Tennessee.

Fisher gained a patent on a new kind of typewriter, the Fisher Book Typewriter, which could type in bound books. Remember typewriters? They were those archaic machines with keys that caused a lettered arm to push through an ink-soaked ribbon to put letters and words on paper. To speak in today's language: "delete" meant you painted over your mistakes with white-out, "save" meant you pulled the finished paper out and put it somewhere safe and "spell check" meant you actually looked up words in a handy dictionary. "Cut and paste" was a literal term. Looking back, I don't know how we made it.

But typewriters were cutting edge machines a hundred years ago. Fisher's company operated for a time in Athens, before being moved to Cleveland, Ohio, and later to Harrisburg, Pennsylvania. Fisher Typewriter Co. won a gold medal award for the book typewriter at the 1898 Trans-Mississippi and International Exposition and Indian Congress in Omaha, Nebraska. An example of Fisher's book typewriter exists in the McMinn County Living Heritage Museum, and the University of Iowa houses one of Fisher's sales brochures in its special collections department.

In 1903, Fisher merged with Elliot & Hatch to produce book typewriters and other machines that could type on a flat surface, such as billing and

R.J. Fisher, *fourth from left*, on a turkey hunt at Whigg Meadows in Monroe County, 1908. *Courtesy of the McMinn County Historical Society.*

accounting records. Again, at the 1904 World's Fair, the Elliot-Fisher typewriter won a prestigious award. By 1908, the company had sold around forty-seven thousand of the book typewriters, and sales continued to climb over the next ten years. By 1921, Elliot-Fisher had developed its Universal Accounting Machine that could add twenty-three columns at one time, which was the largest adding capacity machine of its time.

Through his inventive genius, as well as his knack for business, R.J. Fisher made the Fisher name, and the name of his hometown, famous all over the United States. Fisher himself had become wealthy, and became even more so when Elliott-Fisher was acquired by Underwood Typewriter Company in 1928. The Fisher home in Athens, a bold, two-story structure, was framed picture perfect at the east end of Washington Avenue and was a testament to the Fisher name and reputation. It remained until 1941, when it was torn down to make way for the new First Baptist Church. Two of Fisher's sons, E.G. and R.J. Jr., followed their father's example and were successful in the Athens Hosiery Mill.

But one aspect of R.J. Fisher that seems to speak more of the man himself is revealed in the record and photographs of a hunting trip he took in 1908 into the mountains east of Tellico Plains. The photographs and story of this trip can be viewed online at www.tennesseeoverhill.com. Fisher, along with Dr. James Vaugn, Charles Keith, Beulah McGee and Fisher's two young sons, traveled deep into the mountains to Whigg Meadows and Hooper Bald.

In the photographs, Fisher does not fit the profile of an already successful business owner and nationally recognized inventor. He is simply a father, taking time out of his remarkable life to enjoy a grand adventure with his boys in the Tellico wilderness.

SOLDIER, COWBOY AND SCOUT: "WILD" HARRISON LEWIS

When Harrison Lewis was laid to rest in Liberty Hill Cemetery in McMinn County on a cold Sunday in February of 1934, people from all parts of the country were scratching their heads. For as the sandy, red Liberty Hill soil covered over Lewis's pine coffin, so would the truth about the remarkable man be hidden forever, and leave unanswered questions that linger even today.

He was born in Blount County in 1850, son of Anderson Lewis and his part-Cherokee wife Sarah Ledbetter. Not much is known about Lewis as a young man, but he would later claim to have been a Confederate veteran. By 1870, he was living as a farmer in McMinn County.

At the ripe old age of seventy-two, Lewis wrote his memoirs, and much of what is known of him comes from that source. According to the story told by Harrison Lewis himself, he had quite an adventurous life.

He wrote that he had gone west after 1870, seeking adventure on the new frontier. He alleged a period of service as an army scout, hunting buffalo and chasing Comanche. His service, according to himself, was meritorious and was filled with many a fight and pursuit. He even records that he was wounded by Indians, which resulted in his retirement from the army. He came back to Tennessee, lived in Chattanooga for a time and by 1930 was back in McMinn County.

There are, however, several inconsistencies in Lewis's tales. Many simply don't add up when compared to the historical and military records. He certainly drew a federal pension, but that was for services other than his adventurous claims. What Lewis lacked in humility, he certainly made up for in storytelling.

As an eighty-one-year-old man, he again found some notoriety in 1931 when he was involved in a drunken brawl on a Chattanooga street. During the fight, he cut the throat of his twenty-four-year-old adversary, who later died of the injury. Lewis was arrested, but the court found him to be acting in self-defense. With his name in the papers, Lewis seized the opportunity to again relate his adventures in the Wild West, even claiming to have ridden for a time with General Custer. The old man who had bested an attacker almost a quarter his age seemed to fit the stories he told as a tough frontier scout and Indian fighter.

But three years later, Harrison lost his last fight with pneumonia in Selma, Alabama, and was brought back to McMinn County for his funeral and burial. His obituary in the *Athens Post* declared him "of the fast fading ranks who wore the Blue in the War Between the States" and claimed that he had "led a colorful career during his young manhood, and besides rendering service to his country, he was with Buffalo Bill Cody on the Texas frontier, and old residents here remember many exciting stories he told of his experience."

Who and what Harrison Lewis really was remains a mystery, largely forgotten except for an excellent article by Robert Scott Davis in the January 15, 2006 *Chattanooga News Free Press*. Despite having grown up in the Liberty Hill area, I'd never even heard of Lewis until I read Davis's article.

While Harrison's stories remain, so do the questions. Whoever he was and whatever things Lewis did are lost to darkness and the passage of time, buried with him in a lone grave in Liberty Hill.

EUREKA AND OLD ENGLEWOOD

County Road 480 leaves County Road 500 just south of Englewood, Tennessee, and travels down a short hill before passing over Chestuee Creek. The place is a sleepy creek meadow with a quaint farmhouse and barn, and a passerby today might think it to be nothing more. But 150 years ago, this was the site of a major textile mill that eventually gave birth to the town of Englewood a few miles away.

In 1857, John J. Dixon realized the flowing waters of Chestuee Creek were not just picturesque, but were also profitable. He built a milldam and mill and called the place Eureka Cotton Mills. Dixon founded a tradition of textile production that became central to the economic

A rare photograph of the original Eureka Mill at Old Englewood, probably just after the Civil War. The entire community relocated a few miles north with the coming of the Athens-Tellico Railroad in 1894. A portion of the old mill still stands. *Courtesy of the Englewood Textile Museum.*

The mill town of Englewood was typical of a rural industrial town in this photograph from 1900. *Courtesy of the Englewood Textile Museum.*

Millworkers in Englewood were referred to derogatively as "lintheads." But many adopted the nickname proudly and were lifelong mill employees. Often, several generations of a single family would work the mills. *Courtesy of the Englewood Textile Museum.*

In this northeast view of Englewood in 1910, the railroad depot is at the center, and the school is visible in the background. *Courtesy of the Englewood Textile Museum.*

development of the area, and which remains part of Englewood's industrial base and heritage even today. From raw cotton grown in the creek valleys, Dixon's mill produced yarn and warp products that were shipped all over the East Tennessee area. Dixon had a business partner in Elisha Brient, who in 1875 took over the Eureka Mill operation.

A community sprang up around the mill, including a mill store, a blacksmith, a post office and homes for the workers. During the Civil War, Eureka Mills even issued its own paper money, or script, that could be used in the company store. The mill town was known as Eureka Mills, and until 1894 continued a thriving business under Brient's ownership.

But when the Athens-Tellico Railroad was built just north of the mill village, the Brients saw a better opportunity to ship their goods. The entire village began to relocate to the railroad, a new town sprang up along with the new mill and the new town was called Tellico Junction. A few years later, the name was changed again to Englewood to reflect the area's trees that reminded some of the forest told about in the old Robin Hood stories.

In 1905, the Louisville and Nashville Railroad was built, and intersected the Athens-Tellico Railroad at Englewood, providing a more direct north-south shipping route for the mills that continued to spring up in Englewood. Besides men's "union suits" and underwear, the mills also began producing hosiery. The Englewood Manufacturing Company, which made hosiery specifically, was established in 1913.

As was common during the industrial age, mills were noisy and dangerous places for employees to earn a living. This is a view of the interior of Englewood's Eureka Mill. *Courtesy of the Englewood Textile Museum.*

Englewood continued to grow around its mill economy. As they had at Eureka, homes began to spring up in neighborhoods known as "Onion Hill" and "Sock Hill." Churches and a school were built, as were stores and a hotel. Eventually other industries came in the form of bottling works and even a movie theater. Not to be forgotten, the original site of Eureka Mills is dimly remembered as "Old Englewood." Part of the old mill remains today.

The millworkers were, as a rule, whites who also raised small home gardens to supplement their incomes. They worked in the loud and often hot mills with lint floating in the air, and were called, with some derogation, "lint-heads." Over the years, sons and daughters would come to work alongside their parents, and sometimes two or three generations would continue the "family business" as millworkers. The women worked in the spinning rooms where the thread was prepared. Men worked as supervisors and operated the machines. Even young boys and girls could find jobs, and at times a child's income might support an entire family.

Both the Eureka Cotton Mills and the Englewood Manufacturing Company closed during the Depression, forcing many workers to find work in government relief programs. But when World War II came, the need for hosiery reopened the mills. After the war, the mills were part of the National Clothing Center that sent clothing to help rebuild war-torn Europe.

As the twentieth century drew to a close, so did the mill industry in Englewood, as cheaper labor and products that could be found elsewhere closed nearly all of the mills. But evidence of the twenty-four mills that once called Englewood home still remains in the Englewood Company Store and Textile Museum, which celebrates the common millworkers who were such an integral part of Englewood's history.

KEITH MANSION

It is one of Athens's most recognized homes, a Greek Revival–style "mansion," as it is still called. A tall and imposing brick house with columned portico and circular drive, and with its grounds manicured and shaded by trees over a century and a half old, the house brings back memories of wealth and influence from times long since past. It is known as the Keith mansion.

Few people realize that the present home is actually the second house to occupy this site. Once, another large brick home stood here, built in the early 1800s for Dr. Augustus Pryor Fore (later, this name became Foree). This home burned, and a new house was afterward constructed in 1858 by Thomas Crutchfield for Mr. Fore's daughter, Sarah Anne Penelope Fore,

Keith mansion with original portico, built in 1854. Union soldiers tore the portico down for firewood in 1863. It remains Athens's most recognized historic home. *Courtesy of the McMinn County Historical Society.*

and her new husband, Colonel Alexander Hume Keith. Colonel Keith was the son of Judge Charles Fleming Keith, a noted jurist who for a long time held a seat on the circuit court bench in Tennessee and was related to U.S. Supreme Court Chief Justice John Marshall. The elder Keith had resided at his home at Elmwood, which is now part of the Mayfield Farm just north of Athens.

The new Keith home took six years to complete, as it was delayed due to the various armies passing through the area during the Civil War. Its walls are sixteen inches of solid brick, made on site by Crutchfield's slaves, who were master brick makers. The place was a common campsite for soldiers, as it offered good water and broad fields to set up tents, and was at the same time only a mile from town. It is said that the house was damaged due to portions of the portico being torn down and used in the soldiers' campfires. The home itself was likely used by officers, as well as for a hospital for sick and injured soldiers.

Sarah Anne Keith began a long tradition of association between the Keith family and the Methodist church in Athens by donating property to build a parsonage, and she is said to have conducted Bible studies in her home. One of the ministers who often preached at the Methodist church was

William G. Brownlow, a stout Unionist and later governor and U.S. senator from Tennessee. It is curious to wonder how well Brownlow's Unionism and the Keiths' Confederate sympathies meshed under the Methodist cloth. The Keiths remained a part of the Methodist church through its division before and after the Civil War, and when the old church burned in 1949, the new building constructed near the old Keith home was renamed Keith Memorial.

For many generations, the home remained in the Keith family. Today it is operated as a bed-and-breakfast by Chef Paul Carideo and his wife, Melonie. Their Keith Mansion website describes its atmosphere and preservation.

> *The original wide plank pine floors, marble fireplace hearths and mantles, four panel, pegged doors with transoms, woodwork and molding are all still intact and functioning. The hand carved pegged cherry handrail on the lovely hall staircases is another fine example of nineteenth century carpentry.*
>
> *The home underwent major renovations in 1939, adding new wiring, a furnace, and the grand portico that now dominates the front façade along with four huge Tuscan columns which was the original Crutchfield plan in the 1850s. The Keith Mansion stayed in the Keith family for almost 100 years.*

The home remains as Athens's most noted antebellum mansion. Periwinkle, sometimes called graveyard grass, grows mysteriously on the east side of the home, and often brings questions from curious visitors. The old house reminds those who pass of the romance and lost way of life of the old South, of slaves and plantations, of prosperity and conflict and of religion and contradictions that make up the fibers of our history.

THE MULE TROLLEY

On a hot August day in August of 1887, public transit came to McMinn County.

Of course, the term "public transit" did not exist then, and although efforts to provide public transit in metro areas today are based largely upon fuel conservation, pollution reduction and relieving traffic congestion, the public transit introduced in Athens that day was centered more upon connecting the downtown area with a new industrial/residential development in North Athens. And since today's innovative propane and electric transit also did

Athens's trolley car and mules, pictured in front of the car barn at the present site of Trinity Methodist Church. *Author's collection.*

not exist, the Athens experiment had to depend upon another type of propulsion system: mule power.

Money was plentiful in those days due to a post–Civil War economic boom and the Industrial Revolution that was causing changes all over the country. There was lumber to be shipped out of the mountains near Tellico Plains, and copper ore needing to be mined and transported from Polk County. An entire "new city" was being planned just north of Athens with its own housing, mills, railroad station, hotel and school. A railcar was seen as a useful tool to move people around, as well as a status symbol of a growing and prosperous area.

According to a report by David Stienberg of Chattanooga, the Athens Street Railway was intended to connect Courthouse Square with the Athens Mining and Manufacturing Company properties in the area of present Woodward Avenue. On that first day, the company consisted of one mile of twenty-pound T-rail laid directly in the middle of the city streets, one railcar and two mules. The car had been purchased from the Feigel Car Company in new Utrech, New York, and shipped by train to Athens. Within a year or so, the line was extended another half-mile, and later the entire enterprise would involve two and a half miles of track, over which operated two cars. Wagon service had long existed to haul people and goods to and from the East Tennessee and Georgia/Southern Railroad depot, but this was the first time that more than six or eight people could ride in a single vehicle to several points on an established route.

Annex Hotel under construction on the downtown Athens square in 1898. Trolley tracks are visible in the right foreground. *Courtesy of the McMinn County Historical Society.*

Each car had a roof with open sides, which could allow for an uncomfortable trip on cold, windy or rainy days. A car held twenty people, and the line operated out of a car barn on or near the present site of Trinity Church. Here cars were serviced and mule teams stabled until it was their turn to pull the railcar. The Neptune Livery Stable also operated there, continuing into the twentieth century as a place for persons to keep their horses and wagons while they went about their business in town. The stable was later owned by the Foster family, whose home on Washington Avenue is now Majestic Mansion Bed-and-Breakfast. Horses and mules were dependable as transportation and draft animals, but they brought about their own set of problems. More than one late nineteenth-century newspaper editorial complained about the manure in the streets, as well as the mud and dust, not to mention the smell, generated by horses and mules.

The line ran around Courthouse Square and up Jackson Street, where it turned east onto Woodward, then past the Grand Hotel that stood near the present Woodward Avenue Church of God. The line took in the downtown area, the college, the railroad station and several other points that were both public and private. Photographs still exist of the cars and the barn, as well as the tracks. But like most of the developments associated with the Athens Mining and Manufacturing venture, the streetcar seems to have been out of business by 1900. The tracks remained for a while as a reminder of the venture.

A few years later, the first motorcar bounced into town, followed soon by many more. The automobile brought a newer and faster way to travel and move goods, and also brought about a new symbol of wealth and ability. With the streetcar went the need for livery stables, and it was the automobile that drove the need for paved streets and roads. Finally, even the last vestige of the once unique Athens Street Car Company disappeared when the old tracks were removed when Athens's streets were paved around 1926.

Chapter 6

POLITICS

I t is said that "All politics are local." In rural East Tennessee counties this is especially true, and Athens holds the record of perhaps the best known local political event in the twentieth century. Even a parking space can hold a political history in a small town.

LOOKING PAST THE "BATTLE"

Interest continues to increase about McMinn County's most notable incident: that of Election Day, August 1, 1946, known to most as the "Battle of Athens." A recent historic sign marks the location of the incident of a brief armed siege at the old downtown McMinn County Jail, when GIs just back from World War II removed what they felt was an entrenched political machine. Sixty years later, curiosity still runs deep over this local incident that put McMinn County on newspaper covers all over the nation and even brought about a response from Eleanor Roosevelt. My good friend Paul Willson shares my interest in the "Battle of Athens," but his is as much a personal interest as it is historical. "We Americans like our history written like Greek tragedies," he says most eloquently. "We like our villains to be evil and our heroes on white horses." I agree. This oversimplification is an error easily made, and one that has probably caused the incident to be spoken of as it has over the years, which is as little as possible. For as exciting as that August evening was, the bullets that flew that Election Day were only the flashpoint of a long and drawn-out series of events that had begun eighty years earlier.

When the Civil War ended over 140 years ago, the Reconstruction governments of the former Confederate states were almost entirely Republican. Between the lasting animosity between former foes and the effects of poorly written laws, combined with the inherent symptoms of party politics, problems were easily born. For example, in Tennessee at that time the county sheriff was endowed with much more power than is enjoyed now. Nearly all fines collected by a sheriff on any arrest went to the sheriff's own accounts. This encouraged feegrabbing by arresting as many people as possible, especially on the weekends, when more fines could be garnered, as well as the cost of a prisoner's meal at the jail. To make matters worse, politics entered into the arrest process. Those persons who did not support the Republican sheriff were sure to face intimidation if they tried to vote him out. Speaking in the rhetoric of the day some years after the Civil War at a gathering at Cog Hill, Thomas J. Dement said, "The Republican Party is so corrupt the man in the moon has to hold his nose while passing over." Newspapers from the years after the Civil War tell of many an Election Day fraught with fights and shootings on both sides of the ticket. Many lives were lost on these Election Day battles. But Republicans held most of the power by establishing political machinery. This continued successfully, at least until 1930.

With the Great Depression came a great deal of finger pointing among political parties, and the rise of President Franklin Delano Roosevelt, his New Deal policies and the Democratic Party. Not to sound too general, but it was basically the Democrats' turn at being in charge after sixty years at suffering under the Republican machines. This was accomplished by the Democrats adopting the very same machine system that had held them in check. It might even be said that Democrats perfected the machine system, as imperfect as it was. Turnabout is fair play, or so the phrase goes. To say that all was bad under the Democrat administrations across the state would be a lie; Memphis enjoyed better standards of living and a better job market than it ever had. McMinn County also flourished, and county teachers drew more pay than ever. In some ways the machine system was positive, and in other ways it clearly was not. But one thing is for sure: it was the way that both major political parties did business for eight decades.

After the young servicemen had fought hard to change the world during World War II, they returned home with a spirit of change they intended to put into their communities. McMinn County was no different than many other places across the country: youthful idealism came into direct conflict with old politics. The GIs who returned from Europe and the Pacific were less concerned over what political party was in control than over what they deemed as right and wrong. In their eyes, political machinery had severe faults, and it was time for it to go. Looking back over sixty years, incidents such as the Battle of Athens resulted in ends that seem to justify the means. Flawed laws and old ways of operating government were given up, and a new system of local government in Tennessee was born, literally, in McMinn County as a result of the Election Day "Battle."

Ballots lie scattered across the floor of the old McMinn County Jail. GIs challenged an established political machine. These ballots were believed to have been stolen by GIs, which prompted the Battle of Athens. *Courtesy of the McMinn County Living Heritage Museum.*

Under the control of GI party members, the bullet-ridden McMinn County Jail held its former deputies as prisoners. *Courtesy of the McMinn County Living Heritage Museum.*

It is tempting to consolidate the "Battle of Athens" into one tumultuous evening, but to do so robs our history of its deeper truths. To understand the "why" of an event is often much more interesting than the "how." I hope that such truths can still come to light, as many people who were present or witnessed this event are now in the twilight of their lives. For the real story of our short "battle" is long lasting, and is a tale of a strong community that can put conflict behind us for the greater good of our way of life. Whatever side one takes over this issue, one thing is certain: McMinn County is a better place because it happened, and we are a better people because of how we learned from it.

The lesson is that we need not forget that history is simply a record of what was once hoped for. The future is where that hope remains.

Another Hot August Election Day

In August 2006, Tennesseans went to the polls across the state to exercise our right to vote and elect our representatives and public officials. Some counties experienced closely contested races for major offices, but in McMinn County, only a few races were contested, and many feared that voter turnout would be low. For the most part, Election Day of 2006 saw citizens making their way to the polls and quietly casting ballots on new digital machines. Some watched the returns after the polls closed, and the hot August day passed without notice in McMinn County.

But sixty years ago that week, in 1946, McMinn County was far from quiet. For many months prior to Election Day, August 1, the political rhetoric had filled newspapers, provided fodder at breakfast diners and restaurants and served to provoke both anger and fear. Something was going on all over Tennessee and the South, had been going on for some time, and winds of change were sure to stir something up. Many wondered where it would happen, and some cast their bets on McMinn County. Reporters from far-off cities took up residence in boardinghouses in both Athens and Etowah. Signs sprang up. Rallies were held. Politics had always been as dear to McMinn Countians as their religion, but they had always been able to get beyond those differences once elections were over. With such a charged atmosphere, with antagonistic speeches, accusations and newspaper ads, it was wondered if friendships and family relationships could survive.

Looking back today, it is often portrayed as only a sheriff's race, which is far from the truth. Indeed, Knox Henry was challenging Paul Cantrell for the office, but pretty much every county official's office was being challenged. Although most, if not all, incumbents were Democrats, it is incorrect to draw the conclusion that battle lines ran along those of political parties. This election was something else entirely: it was about different philosophies, and it was about different ideas.

There were many factors that would affect the outcome of Election Day, August 1, 1946. First of all, it was miserably hot. No air conditioning existed then, only open windows and a few electric fans. The heat only fueled the anxiety of both citizens and political opponents. And the heat was always there: at breakfast, at noon, in the evenings, at night; there was no escaping it.

Geography and infrastructure both played a role. Situated sixty miles from Knoxville and Chattanooga, with no interstate highways and only the narrow, winding, two-lane Lee Highway connecting them, Athens, Etowah and McMinn County were far removed from much of the influences of the bigger cities. McMinn had little industry, still had wooden bridges over most creeks, nearly all roads were dirt, a large majority of people had no telephone and in most houses having electricity meant you had one light bulb in the front room. The bill for this service became known, logically to rural customers accustomed to only firelight, as the "light bill."

And then there were the people. The adult and elderly generation had heard their own parents speak of living through slavery, the Civil War and Reconstruction. Over the previous forty years, they had seen their county evolve from pig trails to decent roads, from muddy city streets to concrete and streetlights. Why, an entire town had been conceived and born at Etowah that rivaled even old Athens in power and grandeur.

Unfortunately, laws and politics had not evolved as quickly. Many things were still done the old way. The ways and means of government were easily manipulated, and both political parties had enjoyed the benefits of political machinery to hold their power. Across the South, a good portion of people felt it was the way to continue, while others believed it was time for something new. This element of change was bred in a new generation, in those fresh from the battlefields of a World War. They had youth, vitality and ideas that clashed with the establishment. An election, perhaps the most basic of all American freedoms, was their opportunity to flex their muscles. When the hazy summer sun rose that morning, few could foresee the events that were about to take place. Ballots would be cast, and so would blows. Verbal exchanges would take place, and so would gunshots. But that sunrise would be the last of its kind. Every other sunrise over McMinn County since that day has risen over a new county, a new government and a new people.

Now, on a hot summer election day more than sixty years later, in our excitement to relate those events around the sound of gunshots, of villains, heroes and stories of revolt that were told by sources other than ourselves,

Shaken Athenians view overturned cars and the bullet-ridden McMinn County Jail on White Street the day following the Battle of Athens, August 1, 1946. *Courtesy of the McMinn County Living Heritage Museum.*

The Carnegie Library in Etowah was also the scene of some intense moments during the tumultuous McMinn County election of 1946. *Courtesy of the McMinn County Living Heritage Museum.*

we neglect to recall that it was ideas that clashed that day in 1946, not just people. And ideas, my friends, are what this country is all about.

No matter what political stand one might have adhered to that day, we all came out a little wiser. The bitterest of political enemies found ways to heal. They knew then that the real story was not defined by shootouts or gun ownership, by politics or revolutions, but simply by the fact that we went forward. Life went on. Hopefully, our reaction to our own history has set an example for the rest of the world. We may not like to talk about it, but the events of August 1, 1946, made us all better.

Parking Spaces, Pigeons and Politics

Be it far from me to spread rumors, but I heard an interesting story some time ago that illustrated how politics work in small Southern towns. The story I heard was quite humorous, and was confirmed recently after doing a little research and interviewing.

The following took place in the mid-1970s in a rural Tennessee county, and is recorded in the minutes of the county commission under a section titled "Damage to Courthouse." The record went on to say how the county manager (the office now known as county mayor) had complained in a meeting of county government that the local city police chief had been shooting pigeons off the top of the courthouse, causing several bullets to strike and damage the courthouse cupola. The police chief had acknowledged shooting pigeons off the courthouse, as well as in other areas of town. It was also recorded that no permission had been given for anyone to be shooting pigeons off the courthouse. The record ended by saying the damage had been assessed and a bill would be sent to the local city government for payment of damages. It was interesting to note that there were no criminal charges filed against the chief.

While amusing, the tale didn't end with the official record. While speaking with some persons who were knowledgeable about the event, the following tale emerged:

All counties in East Tennessee have courthouses, and most have dedicated parking spaces that are reserved for county officials. This perk can often cause a bit of a conflict between county government and city government, due to the fact that city streets don't belong to the county. The "reserved parking spaces" are, at best, simply a goodwill gift from a city to a county. Generally this agreement works well enough, but sometimes it doesn't.

Several years ago in a certain county in East Tennessee, the county manager wanted his own parking space in front of the courthouse. The city mayor said no. No matter how much the county manager pleaded, argued and demanded, the city mayor wouldn't hear of it. One of the mayor's biggest supporters in the denial of the request was the city police chief. The chief made it clear to the county manager on more than one occasion that there was no way he would ever get a free parking space around the courthouse. To make matters worse, the county manager often received parking tickets and was once threatened with arrest if he did not pay them. The county manager knew he was powerless to get what he wanted, so he paid his tickets and continued his request.

One evening the county manager was approached by a maintenance worker, who told him that while he had been working late one evening, he had heard the sounds of gunfire outside the courthouse. Peering out his window, he saw the city police chief standing on the corner across the street, firing his duty weapon at the top of the building at the pigeons that had roosted there. The next day, the maintenance worker found several bullet holes and some broken stained glass in the courthouse cupola, which had led him to report the incident to the county mayor. With a mixture of anger and curiosity, the county manager sent for the police chief.

When confronted with the witness's report, the police chief confessed and apologized profusely. But the county manager wasn't ready to accept the apology—at least not until he had worked out an agreement with the chief and the mayor's office. The public record only told part of the story.

What happened afterward helped me to understand why there had been no record of criminal charges filed in the incident, and gave me a whole new insight on how politics sometimes works. Not only did the local city government pay for the damages, but within a few days there was a brand new reserved parking space for the county manager in front of the courthouse.

McMinn County's Declaration of War

It was December 8, 1941, when noted attorney E.B. Madison stood up in the courtroom of the old McMinn County Courthouse. Madison, then an elderly man, held a piece of paper in his hands and cleared his throat as the crowd before him drew silent. He held up the paper and adjusted his eyes, and then he began to read a resolution in support of the declaration of war that had been made only hours earlier by President Franklin Delano Roosevelt against Japan and Germany.

When he was finished, Madison told someone that his voice wasn't as strong as it had been in 1898. For this was not the first time Madison had read a declaration of war.

Forty-three years earlier, on April 28, 1898, the United States had declared war with Spain, in large part in response to the explosion of the battleship *Maine* in Havana Harbor. But McMinn County, wishing to set an example for the rest of the country, was on that day "technically" already at war with Spain, and had been for two weeks. During the county court session in mid-April, the McMinn County Court had met and drafted, more or less, a declaration of war with Spain. It read:

> *Whereas, the people of Cuba are struggling to achieve that liberty which is the gift of Almighty God and the heritage of a free and enlightened people.*
>
> *Therefore, be it resolved by the County Court of McMinn County, Tennessee, that we recognize in the struggling Cuban patriots a liberty loving people who must be free and we recommend to our representatives in Congress irrespective of party that they take such actions as will intervene for the independence of Cuba, the avenging of the Battleship Maine with its crew of American sailors, and the speedy overthrow of Spanish tyranny on this side of the Atlantic and we further declare the independence of Cuba.*

The action of the McMinn County Court (forerunner of the present county commission) was certainly patriotic and determined in its efforts to show support for national action against aggression. Even now, we take pride in the support of our armed forces who serve overseas in the war that our country is presently engaged in. However, with all this history in mind, an interesting fact becomes clear.

Over one hundred years later, even though our federal government has long since made peace with Spain, McMinn County has never officially ended its conflict with Spain. So, at least on paper, McMinn County remains at war with Spain.

Not to alarm our area's Hispanic community, but are we still taking prisoners of war? Are there some hundred-year-old McMinn Countians still fighting on some battlefield in Spain? Were our allies in Monroe, Polk and Meigs Counties in this with us? Isn't it about time we ended this conflict?

Perhaps, according to an idea presented by Judge Carroll Ross, we should contact the Spanish ambassador and formally declare all hostilities between McMinn County, Tennessee, and the nation of Spain to be officially ended. Maybe even sign a treaty. The Spanish delegation and the McMinn County delegation could all meet at Mayfield's Visitors Center, and we could call it the Treaty of Vanilla. There could be a parade with bunting and confetti to celebrate "Peace in Our Time."

There really remains only one question to make all of this happen: Is Spain finally ready to surrender?

Chapter 7

THE CHEROKEE

McMinn County's rich Cherokee heritage remains an important part of its history. Cherokee names still label creeks, valleys, hills, rivers and businesses. We will never be able to part with this sometimes proud, sometimes regretful portion of our history.

The Murder Case that Doomed the Cherokee

The original McMinn County Courthouse, the first to stand on the present town square in Athens in southeast Tennessee, is described as a two-story brick structure that was built in 1823 by the construction firm of Cleage and Crutchfield. Based on surviving evidence of the firm's designs, it was likely a plain-looking building, with strong, square lines, with no porch or façade. This is only a guess, as no photographs survive of the structure, which was torn down in 1875.

No doubt many cases were heard in the courtroom in the old courthouse; several records still exist of those legal matters. But of all the judicial proceedings in early McMinn County, one stands out as having the most far-reaching effect on both McMinn County and the state of Tennessee, if not the entire country. For there was one murder case that was tried initially in McMinn County that set the stage for the eventual removal of the Cherokee nation on what became known as the Trail of Tears.

The crime for which the trial was held took place on August 23, 1834. John "Jack" Walker Jr. was the son of an affluent Cherokee of the same name who operated a large farm and ferry in Calhoun on the Hiwassee River at the edge of the Cherokee nation. Jack Walker was an educated half-breed, the husband of two wives: one white and one Indian. As a member of the Removal Party, Jack Walker believed that the only way for his people to maintain their independence was to sell their ancestral lands and move to the federal reservations west of the Mississippi. This had caused quite a bit of concern among many Anti-Removal Cherokee, even to the point that some called for the assassinations of the Removal Party members, including Jack Walker.

Walker was also a constable, and a few months earlier he had allegedly caught an illegal shipment of whiskey being transported between the Hiwassee and Conasauga River in north Georgia. He confiscated the whiskey and upbraided the two men who were transporting it. The two men were also Cherokee half-breeds, two brothers whose names were James Foreman and Anderson Springston.

On this particular August evening of 1834, Jack Walker was returning from a council at Red Clay near the Tennessee-Georgia line, headed to his house in Walker Valley in present-day Bradley County, Tennessee, along with a companion, Dick Jackson. Without warning, James Foreman and Anderson Springston ambushed the two men from behind a large tree alongside the road. Jackson was unharmed, but Walker received a bullet in his left breast. He was taken home, and after lingering for nineteen painful days, he finally died on September 11.

Foreman and Springston were apprehended by Sheriff Spence Beavers and taken to the McMinn County Jail in Athens. Their trial began November 4, 1834, when they appeared before the Honorable Judge Alexander Keith. Attorney Spencer Jarnigan led the defense council. Samuel Frazier was the prosecuting attorney.

Without delay, Jarnigan argued that the case should be dismissed, claiming that the 1833 law under which the defendants were charged was unconstitutional. He went on to say it was entirely improper for the McMinn County Court to hear the case, as the incident had taken place within the limits of the Cherokee nation, which at the time was the land south of the Hiwassee River. Previous treaties, Jarnigan argued, specifically said that while the Cherokee lived in Tennessee, they were a sovereign and independent nation, and they could not be tried in a state court for a crime committed within the boundaries of their nation. Only the Cherokee laws applied to the incident, not the laws of Tennessee. After a three-day trial, Judge Keith ruled in favor of the defendants and dismissed the case. Frazier almost immediately filed an appeal with the Tennessee Supreme Court. Foreman and Springston were both remanded to the McMinn County Jail, from which they briefly escaped in April of the next year.

Foreman and Springston's key point of their defense, the question of Cherokee rights versus state courts, would also turn out to be the key to the end of the Cherokee nation. Sitting in Knoxville was a Supreme Court judge who had a personal interest in the outcome of the case, and was willing and able to turn that key.

In the early days of Tennessee's Supreme Court, the court met at three different locations: Sparta, Nashville and Knoxville. In the June term of 1835, the court met to hear its cases in the Knoxville district, among which was the Foreman-Springston murder appeal. On the bench were Judges Jacob Peck, Nathan Green and John Catron.

After hearing the merits of the appeal, the Supreme Court nullified the McMinn County Court's 1834 decision to dismiss the murder charge against Foreman and Springston by a vote of two to one. The Supreme Court ruled that the Cherokee were not an independent nation, and could be tried in state courts. This was a critical decision, because the Supreme Court was ignoring nearly all previous decisions that had upheld the rights of the Cherokee. It is interesting to understand why this happened, and to know the motives of Judge John Catron.

Catron was a longtime judge who was often known for his rulings based less on law than on religious convictions. Previous to the Foreman-Springston case, Catron had nearly always ruled in favor of Cherokee rights, and had recognized the independence of the Cherokee nation, as well as the authority of Cherokee government and Cherokee courts. A few years earlier he had ruled that the Cherokee were a nation that had "acknowledged rights; which...have been respected...and the courts of justice are bound to regard."

But by 1835, events had changed on a national scale, and so had Catron's ideas. This was due in no small part to the fact that Catron was a close friend and supporter of none other than President Andrew Jackson. Catron had a long history of working to advance Jackson's career and policies, and in 1835 there were few other policies as important to Jackson as the removal of the Indians to the West.

In his opinion issued in the Foreman-Springston case, Catron ignored his previous rulings and said, "Neither our theory or our practice has ever allowed to the Indians any political right extending beyond our authority." In effect, the court ruled that the Cherokee were a conquered people, and as such were not a sovereign nation; their laws did not override the laws of the state. This also implied that their legal claims to their lands were essentially voided. Judge Green concurred with Catron; only Judge Peck dissented. The murder case was then appealed to the United States Supreme Court.

But there is no record of the Foreman-Springston case ever being heard by the U.S. Supreme Court, or ever again in McMinn County. This fact remains a bit of a mystery. Either the record vanished or the case was simply forgotten. Either could be true, for within six months of Catron's ruling the United States government agent convened an unauthorized council with members of the Removal Party at New Echota while the Anti-Removal

The grave of young Elizabeth Ross, niece of Cherokee Chief John Ross. Elizabeth died in Calhoun while her family prepared to embark on the Trail of Tears. Her grave remains as a symbol of one of East Tennessee's darkest hours. *Photo by Stephanie Guy.*

Party was on its way to Washington. Even though most of the Cherokee were against removal, the Treaty of New Echota, the final removal agreement, was signed on December 29, 1835, and was approved the next day by only a minority of Cherokee. The deed was done.

So the point of defense by Foreman and Springston, the issue of Cherokee laws versus state laws, was used by a politically motivated judge to doom the Cherokee. The decision of John Catron paved the way for history, resulting in the removal of the Cherokee. Within three years, Jackson's policy had been fulfilled, and the Cherokee were gone.

For more information on the Foreman-Springston Trial, see Theodore Brown Jr.'s "The Formative Period of the Supreme Court of Tennessee, 1796–1835." In *A History of the Tennessee Supreme Court*, edited by James W. Ely Jr. Knoxville: University of Tennessee Press, 2002.
Holdings of the Tennessee State Library and Archives, Nashville, TN.
McMinn County Historical Society and Archives, Athens, TN.

General Wool and the Trail of Tears

A few years ago, the National Parks Service researched and marked the different routes taken by the Cherokee during their removal to Oklahoma in the late 1830s, which are known collectively as the Trail of Tears. But while the research and trail designation were certainly well done, some parts of the story were left out, including the routes through McMinn and Monroe Counties. Records strongly indicate that a large number of Cherokee in southeast Tennessee and Western North Carolina were marched through Tellico Plains, down present-day Mecca Pike and Highway 39, past the areas of present-day Englewood and Etowah, down Zion Hill Road and into Athens before moving south toward Fort Cass at Calhoun. Additional research done over recent years by Kenneth Langley has unearthed the actual records of these operations, specifically the military papers of General John Ellis Wool, which are housed in the New York State Library in Albany.

General Wool was stationed in Athens from 1836 to 1837 as the commanding officer of a body of U.S. troops charged with gathering up Cherokee who had refused to leave their lands after the removal treaty was signed in 1835. Wool records that he had his headquarters in the "old Bridges Hotel," and receipts generated by Wool were made out to James S. Bridges, the owner. Several hotels were once operated in Athens under the Bridges name, but this one in particular is traced through Wool's records and old newspapers to the present site of the old Robert E. Lee Hotel on the corner of West Madison and Jackson Streets. The September 13, 1850 *Athens Post* carried an advertisement for George Mayo operating a hotel in the "large brick tavern on the public square formerly occupied by James S. Bridges." The March 8, 1925 *Chattanooga Times* carried a photograph and editorial of the "old Bridges Hotel" just before it was torn down to make way for the Robert E. Lee. The old hotel had been built by Samuel Cleage in the early 1830s. This particular site would have been well suited for Wool's headquarters, as the stagecoach stop for Athens was also at this spot.

Several bills and receipts are contained in General Wool's papers for room, board and other necessities, as are records of federal funds being deposited in the Farmer's Bank of Athens, which was located on the present-day site of All-Star Sports, to support Wool's operations. His troops were garrisoned in a camp a short distance away, near the "Mathews Mill," which at that time was just across Eastanaulee Creek near the Jackson Street Bridge.

Parties of Cherokee were, in fact, marched into Athens during this fateful time. In J.M. Sharp's *Recollections and Hearsays of Athens*, Colonel C.G. Samuels was recorded as having been a small child living at the old Forest Hill School near the present E.G. Fisher Library when "two men on horses dashed up to the front Gate and ordered my father, his brother, and my mother's brother to get their guns and proceed to Athens, then a small village, to protect it from Indian attack as several hundred of the Indians had escaped [from the army stockades] and were headed toward Athens." Later it was apparent that the Cherokee were simply marching through on their way to Calhoun. In *History of the Connector Road*, accounts are given of Cherokee being marched past Zion Hill Church south of Englewood during this time, headed toward Athens en route to Fort Cass.

Because Wool was sympathetic to the Cherokee's plight and had intervened on their behalf in some incidents in Alabama, Wool was relieved of his duties in June of 1837 by Colonel Lindsay, who took command and also made his headquarters at the Bridges Hotel. It appears that Lindsay continued the removal operations until they were completed in 1838.

The dark days of the Trail of Tears are remembered today along the paths marked by the National Park Service, and with the support of Congressman Zach Wamp new designations will hopefully be added to expand the history of the Cherokee removal, including the path through Athens and the headquarters of General Wool. In addition to the John Walker murder trial held in 1834 in the McMinn County Courthouse, McMinn County can lay claim to two important events that made up the tragic story of the Trail of Tears.

General John E. Wool maintained his Athens headquarters in the Bridges Hotel during his involvement in the Cherokee removal from 1836 to 1837. During the time it was in operation, the hotel served as a stagecoach stop for travelers from New York to New Orleans, and was also utilized as quarters for General William T. Sherman during the Civil War. The hotel is pictured here with its two-story veranda on Jackson Street. It was demolished in 1926. *Courtesy of the McMinn County Living Heritage Museum.*

JACKSON'S COUNCIL IN CALHOUN, 1817

It must have been hot that June day in 1817, even within the cabin that served as the office of the Cherokee Agency at the frontier settlement at Walker's Ferry on the Hiwassee River, soon to be renamed Calhoun. Inside was a tall, slim man with thick, brown hair, a national hero who many in the area had walked for miles just to catch a glimpse of. He was General Andrew Jackson, hero of the Creek War in 1812 and famous for his defeat of the British in New Orleans in 1815. But on this June day, Jackson was not enjoying his fame and recognition. He stood there, arms crossed over his chest, his brow furrowed, knowing that he had a serious problem on his hands.

He had that year been appointed a commissioner to the Indians by President James Monroe, and had been going from town to town all spring to drum up support for a treaty conference between the Western Cherokee in the Oklahoma Territory and the Eastern Cherokee in Tennessee and Georgia. On June 20, most of the Western chiefs had arrived in the small frontier settlement on the Hiwassee where Chief John Walker operated a large farm, store and ferry. But the Eastern chiefs refused to come. Jackson was deeply angry, because the Eastern chiefs had realized his secret plan:

to persuade them to move West and leave forever their ancestral lands in East Tennessee.

But if Jackson was not happy, he was tenacious. Almost immediately he set upon a new plan, and gathered up some associates he knew and sent them to speak with certain other Eastern chiefs. If he could not get the chiefs he wanted to come, then he would get other chiefs who he could bribe to show themselves. Any chief's signature on a treaty was as good as another, as far as Jackson was concerned. He needed a treaty that would open up land for white settlement and thereby allow the young country of America to grow. Jackson saw no reason why Indians should be allowed to hold on to millions of acres of land simply to hunt on.

For the next week or so, Jackson's agents went through the Cherokee nation, plying the other chiefs with whiskey and promises of bribes and gifts. Slowly, these chiefs began to arrive at the Cherokee Agency until enough were present for Jackson to conduct his business. Also during this time, another notable white man arrived who was intent on seeing the Cherokee give up their land: the Tennessee governor himself, Joseph McMinn.

Jackson, McMinn and General David Meriwether met with the assembled chiefs, many of whom were also men of note, including Glass, Spring Frog, Savanooka and Old Bark. Others had white names, such as John Walker, George Saunders, George Lowry, John McIntosh, John Jolly and James Rogers. Jackson outlined his proposal: the Cherokee should trade all of their eastern lands, acre for acre, for lands west of the Mississippi. All Cherokee claims in Georgia and Tennessee would be given up, and "poor warriors" who chose to emigrate west would be given a "rifle gun, ammunition, a blanket, and a brass kettle or in lieu of the latter a beaver trap." Cherokee who chose to remain would receive a farm of their own and citizenship equal to free blacks.

With many of the Eastern chiefs in the pay of Jackson, the treaty was approved and signed by all those present on July 8, 1817. It was hurriedly sent to Washington for ratification.

Reputable Cherokee leaders who had refused to come to Jackson's council were outraged at what became known as the Jackson-McMinn Treaty. Two of these men, Major Ridge and John Ross, went to Washington to try to stop the passage of the treaty. Much to Jackson's surprise, they succeeded the following December. But again, Andrew Jackson was not the kind of man to take defeat lightly. He had political aspirations, and his eyes were set on a big white house in Washington.

Although it was repealed, the 1817 treaty continued to be enforced, although underhandedly. Over the next few years, the agents of Jackson and McMinn continued to roam the Cherokee nation, offering more bribes and encouragement for the Indians to move west. Some of the Indians took the meager gifts and left, hoping to find a better life out west. Many remained, and through subsequent treaties that sold their lands little by little, they tried to adapt to white culture. But the determined plans Jackson and McMinn made on the banks of the Hiwassee River in 1817 would eventually come to pass, and two decades later, the Cherokee were gone.

INDIAN SUMMER

The last warm days of autumn, typically in early November, provide one last taste of summer before the cold of winter takes hold of our region. It is a yearly weather phenomenon that occurs when a high-pressure system settles itself over the Southeast before being pushed out by arctic winds. We look forward to these days that for over a hundred years have been referred to as "Indian Summer" as one last chance to wear a pair of shorts or take a drive on a sunny day with the top down. But in early America, these were days filled with fervent work and an uncertain dread of lurking danger.

In the late 1700s, when nearly all Americans farmed for sustenance, the last warm days of the year provided the final opportunity to complete the work of harvest. Potatoes were dug and "hilled" to preserve them during the winter, the last of the corn and grain were put in the cribs and the remaining hay was cut and gathered to feed the livestock. All this must be done before the days turned cold and trails and roads turned into muddy quagmires that froze every night and melted every day and never seemed to go dry. These days also might be used to raise a barn, visit neighbors or even make one last trip to a trading post or town to procure the clothing and supplies to get a family through until the spring planting.

But during this time of business, the frontier farmer working in his fields labored with his rifle gun leaning on a nearby tree. Sometimes, two men would work together, one doing the work while the other stood guard with musket primed and loaded, scanning the tree line for any sign, any movement, any sound that would alert them of what they knew was out there: Indians.

The Cherokee also looked forward to the warm time. They, too, took the opportunity to gather the last of the harvest, but they had other work to do as well. With little other choice but to drive encroaching whites from their lands, this was also the last time of the year to take to the warpath. The Cherokee, like many tribes on the frontier, knew that the white farmers were vulnerable as they worked their farms before winter. Few would be able to "fort up" together to defend themselves, as they were too busy attempting

The whites had a name for this time when the Indian raids were not just a possibility, but were a certainty. They called it "Indian Summer." *Photo by Stephanie Guy.*

to finish the harvest. So as the days dawned warmer between the first cool days of fall and the coming cold of winter, the Cherokee gathered around council fires in their towns. Young men talked of scalps they would take as they painted their faces in fearsome streaks of black and red. All night they danced the war dance, each man striking the central war pole with knife and tomahawk and declaring his past exploits against his enemies, both Indian and white. The war song rose up in the smoky darkness of early morning as the men gathered into groups, each with its own captain. Carrying only a handful of corn and their muskets, they disappeared into the orange, gold and red leaves that danced in the autumn breeze.

The whites had a name for this time when the Indian raids were not just a possibility, but a certainty. They called it "Indian Summer." Tales traveled quickly of men found scalped in their fields, of children taken, of women attacked while carrying water from the spring. In cabins sprinkled across remote coves and hillsides, families took care to keep a gun loaded and powder and ball within easy reach, never to step out the door without first looking out, never to walk into the forest alone. Every track, every evening crack of a twig, made one stop in his or her footsteps to listen, to look. Wondering who might be near…

But the warm spell would never last, and soon the cold north wind would bring nightly frost and winter days that kept both the farmer and the warrior in their homes, each smoking his evening pipe after going about his daily business, always mindful of the other and of the coming spring, when their blood and their days would grow warm once again.

ABOUT THE AUTHOR

J oe D. Guy is a nationally published author, syndicated newspaper
columnist, storyteller and historian from East Tennessee. Mr. Guy's
popular syndicated newspaper column "Beyond the Blue Line," published
from 1999 to 2004, was drawn from stories he has collected during his
twelve-year career as a police officer, deputy sheriff, EMT, SWAT team
commander and detective. Writers Club Press published a collection of the
articles, *Beyond the Blue Line: Stories from the Other Side of Law Enforcement*, in
2002. Mr. Guy published *Beyond the Blue Line Volume 2*, his second collection
of sixty-two stories, through PublishAmerica in 2005. His articles on school
safety and officer-community relations issues have appeared in *Community
Policing Exchange* and *Community Links*, and were widely recognized by school
systems and law enforcement agencies across the country.

A student of history, Mr. Guy is also the author of the historical narrative
Indian Summer: The Siege and Fall of Fort Loudoun (The Overmountain Press,
2001), which has received excellent reviews among newspapers, historical

groups and tourism associations. Other historical articles have appeared in *Appalachian Life Magazine*, *Backwoodsman Magazine* and in *McMinn County: A History of Its People*. Mr. Guy was a 2000 and 2002 scholarship winner in both fiction and nonfiction at the Lost State Writers Conference in Greeneville, Tennessee. Since 2004, he has written "Hidden History," a regional history column that continues to grow subscribers in several East Tennessee newspapers.

Currently, Mr. Guy is the assistant to the county mayor and county historian in McMinn County, Tennessee, where he resides with his wife and children.

Please visit us at
www.historypress.net